Eyewitness Auschwitz

THREE YEARS IN THE GAS CHAMBERS

Filip Müller

Literary collaboration by
Helmut Freitag

Edited and translated by
Susanne Flatauer

Foreword by
Yehuda Bauer

IVAN R. DEE
Chicago

Published in Association with the
United States Holocaust Memorial Museum

EYEWITNESS AUSCHWITZ. Copyright©1979 by Filip Müller. Translation copyright by Routledge & Kegan Paul Ltd. All rights reserved. First Ivan R. Dee paperback edition published 1999. For information, address: Ivan R. Dee, Publisher, 1332 North Halsted Street, Chicago 60622. Manufactured in the United States of America and printed on acid-free paper.

Published in association with the United States Holocaust Memorial Museum.

Library of Congress Cataloging-in-Publication Data:
Müller, Filip.
    Eyewitness Auschwitz : three years in the gas chambers / Filip Müller ; literary collaboration by Helmut Freitag ; edited and translated by Susanne Flatauer ; foreword by Yehuda Bauer.
        p. cm.
    ISBN 1-56663-271-4 (alk. paper)
    1. Auschwitz (Concentration camp). 2. World War, 1939–1945—personal narratives, Czech. 3. Müller, Filip. 4. Prisoners of war—Czechoslovakia—Biography. 5. Prisoners of war—Poland—Biography.
    I. Freitag, Helmut. II. Flatauer, Susanne. III. Title.
    D805.5.A96M85 1999
    940.54'7243'094386—dc21   99-32041

Eyewitness Auschwitz

Filip Müller was born in 1922 in Sered, Czechoslovakia. He was deported to Auschwitz in April 1942 where he was assigned prisoner number 29236. He worked as a prisoner in the *Sonderkommando* until the evacuation of the camp in January 1945 and was liberated in May 1945. Afterwards he was unable to work until 1953 when he became an auditor in Prague. Since 1969 he has lived in Western Europe.

Open thy mouth for the dumb in the cause of all
such as are appointed to destruction.

Proverbs 31.8

Contents

Foreword

Filip Müller's book is a unique document indeed: it is the testimony of the only man who saw the Jewish people die and lived to tell what he saw. It is not known exactly how many people were murdered at Auschwitz, but continuing research has led scholars to refine the estimates. Most now agree that the Auschwitz concentration camp complex claimed the lives of approximately 1.1 million people, close to 1 million of whom were Jews. Müller came to Auschwitz with one of the earliest transports from Slovakia in April 1942, and began working in the gassing installations and crematoria in May. He managed to stay alive until November 1944, when the gassings ceased. By a stroke of sheer luck he survived. He saw multitudes come and disappear. He saw the families, the townships and the cities of the Jewish people come, enter the house of death and burn to ashes. He saw a civilization being destroyed by devils in ordinary, human form. He not only saw the martyrs, but also spoke to Satan. He tells his story in a simple, straightforward language. There is no embellishment, no deviation. This is not a work of art. It is a testimony.

It is a testimony also of a human being who decided, at one point, not to suffer any longer and to choose death. In the same simple, matter-of-fact way that he relates the scenes of hell and fire that he witnessed, he tells the story of his attempted suicide, and the ultimate cruelty of the SS guard who prevented it; he tells of the beauty of Yana's death in the horror of the mass murder, perhaps the most poignant story of any Holocaust testimony.

Müller is neither a psychologist nor a historian. Since he first published his memoir in the 1970s, we have learned a great deal about Auschwitz, so that we now know that there are inaccuracies in some of his statistics and diagrams as presented here. As far as these items are concerned, the reader should refer to historical accounts published in the more recent past. These inaccuracies do not detract from the personal story he relates, which is nevertheless of tremendous importance to historians, psychologists, and generations of vicarious survivors, Jewish and non-Jewish: for we are all the survivors of man's madness. Some will notice the lack of successful resistance; some will notice the fact that the author does not mention any case of Jews begging for their lives; some will emphasize the fact that most of the Jews going to the gas chambers had no inkling of what was happening to them; others will analyse the behaviour of the SS murderers. This is a vital testimony, and it will undoubtedly serve as an element in attempting to approach an understanding of the dread that was Auschwitz, although none of us who was not there can cross the threshold of knowledge.

The Jewish people, some thousands of gypsy people and many others were murdered in the gas chambers. Thousands of others were shot. This unembellished telling is a terrible accusation against God and humanity.

Why did Müller not publish his memoir before? He did, in a way. He returned to his Czechoslovak home after the war. A summary of his testimony was included in a book in Czechoslovakia in 1946 (published in English in 1966 as *The Death Factory*, by O. Kraus and E. Kulka). He was moved to write again by the effect of his testimony at the 'Auschwitz trial' at Frankfurt, in 1964. Afterwards he began writing up what he had jotted down, had it translated into German, then looked for a publisher. The result is before us: a shattering, centrally important testimony of the sole survivor of the whole span of the murder operations of the Auschwitz–Birkenau killing centre, of the *anus mundi*. We must contend with Filip Müller's testimony, if we want our civilization to survive.

Professor Yehuda Bauer
Director, International Center for Holocaust Studies
Yad Vashem, Jerusalem

Eyewitness Auschwitz

Chapter 1
No return

It was a Sunday in May 1942. Struggling through the early morning mist, a fitful spring sun shone on the yard of Block 11 where some 500 prisoners had lined up in rows of ten so that they might enjoy their Sunday rest according to established Auschwitz tradition. The sound of a hoarse voice barking orders rang across the yard: it belonged to Vacek, the block clerk*, who was standing at the top of a flight of stairs. From this vantage point he was able to survey every corner of the yard below and bellow out his commands: 'Shun! Caps on! Caps off! Get a move on!' According to the green triangle on his uniform Vacek was a former professional criminal: in this microcosm of absolute evil he ruled supreme.

With eagle eyes he watched to see that his orders were carried out meticulously. At the command 'Caps off!' we whipped our flat caps from our shaven heads and slapped them against our right thighs with the flat of our hands. Unless this produced the whip-cracking sound envisaged by Vacek, the exercise would be repeated until he was satisfied. On this occasion it had already been repeated more than a hundred times. At first glance this tedious drill, not unlike the drilling of army recruits, might appear to be perfectly harmless and nothing out of the ordinary. In fact, it merely served to provide Vacek with the desired pretext for putting prisoners to death.

On this particular Sunday his first victim was a father of four whose right hand was paralysed. Before he became an inmate of Auschwitz he had scraped a living by reciting the Kaddish, the

*All words marked with an asterisk are explained in the Glossary.

1

prayer for the dead, in the synagogue of his native town. It was, of course, quite ludicrous to expect a man with his handicap to execute the 'Caps off! Caps on!' drill correctly. Vacek flung himself on the disabled man and dragged him across the yard. There he stood him with his face to the wall. His next victim was a deaf tailor who had been a fraction of a second late in snapping to attention. The drill continued. Everybody was longing for this monotonous exercise to stop, especially since at long last everything was going like clock-work. But Vacek was not satisfied with only two victims. From out of the ranks of slaves he fetched several more, no longer bothering to look for pretexts. Anything trivial that displeased or irritated him, such as a man's long nose, a pair of spectacles with thick lenses, an ill-fitting cap, was sufficient reason for him to pounce on one unfortunate prisoner after another and line him up against the wall.

For in this place the lame, the blind and the weak would look in vain for mercy or pity. The Ten Commandments, those principles of human conduct, did not prevail here: Auschwitz had its own laws and macabre values. At Auschwitz gold teeth might buy a bowl of turnip soup; at Auschwitz a camp orchestra would play cheerful military music, not only in the morning when the prisoners marched out to work, but also at night when, bruised and battered, they struggled back carrying their dead comrades.

At Auschwitz *Kapos** were given rewards and privileges for reducing the number of men in their working party; how they did this was their own affair. At Auschwitz, in Block 10, women were sterilized while in another block men were castrated. Auschwitz was a place where every European language was spoken; it was also a place where people died, not only from starvation, sickness and epidemics, but from being battered to death, killed by having phenol injected into their heart, or driven into the gas chamber. This wretched piece of land in eastern Europe was under the sway of the SS whose members regarded themselves as the élite of the German nation, a nation which had given to the world not only great writers and composers, but also men like Adolf Hitler. The little Polish town of Oswieczim, which the Nazis called Auschwitz, had been turned into an inferno, and anyone taken there by an unkind fate might regard himself truly forsaken by God and his fellow men.

By now thirty unfortunates had been stood against the wall. Vacek and his underlings ordered them to line up in ranks of five.

And now, behind our backs, began what in Auschwitz went under the name of *sport*. 'At the double! Lie Down! Get up! Lie down! Crawl! Get up! Jump! At the double! About turn!' Like hunted animals the wretched prisoners were harried and chased across the yard. They flung themselves on the ground; crawled on their bellies; leapt up; jumped with arms held out in front; ran about panting and pushing each other in a vain attempt to avoid the blows which were hailing down on them non-stop. They were flushed with exertion, sweat mixed with blood streaming down their faces and necks. Anyone who failed to get up was lost. A blow from a truncheon, followed by several more if necessary, finished him off. Many had already given up: more than half the prisoners were lying motionless on the ground although only twenty minutes had gone by. 'At the double! Lie down! Get up! Jump! Lie down! Get up! Crawl!' Remorselessly command followed command. On the point of complete exhaustion, the remaining prisoners still tried to carry out the orders shouted at them. But before long they too lay still in their zebra-striped uniforms; and were then bludgeoned to death with truncheons. Vacek's bloodthirsty gaze surveyed his harvest of death. Then he wiped the sweat from his forehead, his face distorted by a terrible sneer, his eyes still flashing menacingly. He was visibly pleased with his achievement. No doubt he would have enjoyed finishing off the rest of us in the same way.

Meanwhile the dead bodies had been collected and laid on their backs side by side. Their hands were crossed on their chests and their unseeing eyes seemed to stare questioningly up into the sky. Vacek and his block orderlies turned away, their job well done.

All this time Schlage, the *SS-Rottenführer** on duty, behaved as though the whole gory proceedings did not concern him. A few times he disappeared into the building only to take up his place at the top of the stairs again from where he watched to make quite sure that his block clerk was not flagging in the execution of his duty. In that event he would have abandoned his seeming non-intervention in order to give a demonstration of the true meaning of *sport*, as practised in Auschwitz.

From somewhere among the ranks I could hear the sound of muttering. Somehow I only half-registered it because I was wholly preoccupied with trying not to attract attention. I was then still sufficiently naïve to believe that prompt execution of commands would help to reduce the diabolical torment we were made to undergo. The mumbling now became a clearly audible monologue: 'My God, what on earth is going on here? Prisoners are being killed by fellow prisoners! I'm sure the people in charge know nothing whatever about this. I protest. ...'

There came a fresh flood of commands: 'Shun! Caps on! Caps off! Get a move on!' Vacek collected another four prisoners. This time it did not take long before they, too, were laid out with the other corpses.

'This is intolerable! These are innocent people who are being put to death!'

Surreptitiously I tried to find out who the speaker was. The man who was talking to himself was in fact from my home town of Sered where he had been known as a respected citizen, an excellent lawyer, an authority on Jewish writing, and a man who had consistently sought to soften the harshness of the law for the weak. Like myself he had come to Auschwitz about a month earlier, but unlike me he was one of those who were too slow in coming to terms with the harsh realities of life in a concentration camp. He had failed to realize that in Auschwitz the values and laws which formed the basis of civilization were obsolete. He was firmly convinced that murders were committed by prisoners put in charge of their fellows without the knowledge of SS leaders. It simply did not fit in with his concept of the law that prisoners should be allowed to kill fellow prisoners, and to do this for no reason whatever. He still had not grasped the fact that we were now in a place where there were no laws for prisoners.

At long last this Sunday's drill was coming to an end. We began to fall in for counting. Vacek came down the stairs, barking commands. Then he proceeded to count, first the prisoners who were standing in line, and then the dead who were lying in a corner of the yard. He wrote the result on a slip of paper which he handed to the block senior* at whose command 'Caps off!' we whopped off our filthy caps and clapped them against our right side. For Vacek the simultaneous whip-crack sound which followed was proof that his murderous rehearsal had been well worth while.

Rottenführer Schlage, who all this time was standing in the doorway, now descended the steps with dignity. He received the block senior's report and began to check the figures by stepping up to the left flank of prisoners who were lined up in perfectly straight rows and counting them. There was utter silence, broken

4

only by the twitterings of the swallows darting back and forth above our heads. Suddenly, accompanied by a wave of whispering, the lawyer pushed his way through the ranks and stopped three paces in front of Schlage. Standing smartly to attention, he looked the SS man straight in the eye and declared with sincere indignation: 'Herr Kommandant, as a human being and a lawyer I wish to report that the block clerk' – pointing at Vacek – 'has arbitrarily killed several innocent people. Their corpses are laid out over there. I am convinced that the block clerk has killed these prisoners without the knowledge of either his immediate superiors or the authorities. We have been sent here to work and not to be killed. Monsignor Tiso, President of Slovakia, has himself vouched for our safety. I would therefore request you to have this morning's events investigated and to see that the guilty are duly punished.'

When he had finished making his complaint, one could have heard a pin drop. Astounded at his courage and determination, the prisoners caught their breath and stared at Schlage. He, too, was so surprised by the unexpected conduct of this prisoner that for a time he stood rooted to the spot facing the lawyer. His neck and face grew livid with rage and agitation. The muscles in his face were twitching as he tried to speak. It took a few seconds before he was able to bawl: 'Vacek, come here!'

'At once, *Herr Rottenführer*!' replied Vacek and stood to attention before his master.

'Did you hear what this fucking Jew has been blathering about?'

'I did, *Herr Rottenführer*!' Vacek replied eagerly.

'Then give him what he deserves!' ordered Schlage.

Vacek ran to pick up his truncheon from where he had left it and rushed up to the lawyer. He began to batter him with the truncheon and continued until finally the man dropped dead. Then he hurriedly dragged the body over to the heap of corpses in the corner. As the result of this morning's sporting activities, thirty-five bludgeoned bodies now lay in the yard of Block 11. Schlage, who had observed Vacek's action with satisfaction, now turned to us and asked cynically: 'Anyone else want to make a complaint?'

While his gaze wandered along our ranks, the block senior, at a sign from the *Rottenführer*, ended the midday roll-call by ordering us to fall out. However, our harassment was by no means at an end. Although by now we were exhausted, we stood in line behind the wooden tea vats. Tea should have been issued early in the morning and was now stone cold. We were waiting patiently to be doled out our ladleful but, as it turned out, we were waiting in vain. For Vacek was still tearing round the yard like one demented, gesticulating and shouting that we were entitled to nothing, not even a ladleful of shit, but only – and here he pointed upward – to go up through the chimney. Then he ordered his underlings to pour the tea into the gully-drain. With parched throats and greedy eyes we watched this latest piece of devilry. I could not understand Vacek's action for, after all, he like us was a prisoner. Or, could it be that he was a spy? But surely in that case he would have tried to gain our confidence.

Only much later I learned that Vacek was among the first prisoners in Auschwitz whom the SS appointed as a *Funktionshäftling**. He had joined a group of professional criminals who had undergone special training at the concentration camp of Sachsenhausen. Even at Sachsenhausen these privileged prisoners, who were citizens of the Reich, had been much feared. In May 1940 they had been taken to the newly established concentration camp at Auschwitz where they were to introduce the brutal methods practised in the concentration camps which had existed in Germany ever since 1933. This group of professional criminals and their minions enjoyed a particularly privileged position within the Auschwitz prisoners' self-administration, as well as the esteem of the SS. As camp officials they did not have to do any physical work and, in actual fact, possessed absolute power of life and death over their fellow prisoners. They received more and better food, wore high leather boots and made-to-measure prisoners' garb, besides which they enjoyed many other advantages and privileges. Vacek did not enjoy these for long, though. He died in hospital of typhoid in the autumn of 1942. There was a rumour that after his death male nurses who knew what a sadistic killer he had been, had defecated into his mouth.

Even after the tea had been tipped into the gully-drain we were allowed no peace. Now we were ordered to delouse ourselves. We stood in the yard in small groups searching our shirts which we had stripped off for lice. We were much troubled by lice, and our shirts were crawling with them. Among the many slogans adorning the walls of our block there was one which was not without a certain impertinent cynicism. It warned us that 'one louse may be your death.' This was no exaggeration either, for a louse might infect its host with typhus, a disease which in Auschwitz spelled certain death. Alternatively, any louse discovered during a shirt check might have grave consequences for the prisoner in question. The reason for this could be found in the strange logic of what was known as Auschwitz justice. It argued that any prisoner on whom a louse was found after a delousing order had been issued, had obviously failed or, worse still, refused to obey orders and must therefore be severely punished. To be lousy in Auschwitz was a serious crime and liable to cost a man his life. That water came out of taps only on special occasions or that we prisoners had neither soap nor towel was something in which nobody was interested.

After delousing we were made to soften the stiff leather uppers of our wooden clogs with dirty oil. This was followed by the painful weekly ordeal of a soapless cold-water shave with razors so blunt that the hairs of one's beard were torn out rather than shaved off. The thought that at least they had been spared was all that flashed through my mind as I watched the bearers fling the corpses of the slain on the wooden cart which was to take them away.

Midday, and it was time to eat. The smell of the thin and far from appetizing soup in its steaming cauldron pervaded the yard. Hungrily we watched and sniffed, revived by the thought of food; harassment, torture and violent death were forgotten. All our senses were concentrated on the muck in the cauldrons, a mess of mangel-wurzel and overcooked rotting potatoes which always tasted the same and yet helped us to survive a little longer. Soup was our elixir of life: and any prisoner considered himself very lucky if now and then he managed to wangle a second helping.

Trembling with hunger I stood in the queue waiting for the fatigue orderly to ladle a helping of soup into my red-enamelled tin bowl. I did not bother about a spoon, but drank my soup slowly and noisily, savouring each mouthful. I could feel my vital energy being restored. My greedy tongue searched the bowl for every last drop. Then, thirsty rather than hungry, I went to our barrack to take my compulsory Sunday afternoon rest.

The block orderlies* handed one blanket to every two prisoners sharing a bunk. I lay down on a bunk in the bottom tier near the door. Sharing my bunk and my blanket was a prisoner of about twenty-five or twenty-six. Proximity breeds familiarity: amid the general din we began to talk.

'Where do you come from?' I asked him. '*Comprends pas, camarade,*' he replied.

'Don't you speak German?' I continued.

'*Un petit peu, pas beaucoup,*' he said.

'My name is Filip and I come from Slovakia,' I said very slowly.

He nodded: '*Moi, Maurice de l'Algérie; je suis venu de Drancy.*' Then he added: '*Moi* finished, *par ici* everything finished.' Fumbling for words and gesticulating to make himself understood he tried to explain to me that in his view we were all doomed to go up the chimney.

Suddenly Schlage loomed in the open door: 'If you don't shut up this minute, you fucking bastards, I'll knock your heads off!' he yelled. At once there was silence. Trying to hide their fear the orderlies were running around wielding their sticks and beating any prisoner still standing about onto the nearest empty bunk. Leaning casually against the door-frame Schlage watched his creatures with approval. Once more he surveyed the room, then he turned on his heels and left.

All was silent, only now and then someone coughed or groaned. Most of the prisoners had fallen asleep with exhaustion; many were snoring. I, too, longed for sleep, but sleep would not come, for my tongue clung to the roof of my mouth, my throat was parched: thirst had become a torture. There was absolutely no point in trying to reach the tap. For one thing it was fraught with danger, and besides more often than not there was no water there, anyway.

My neighbour suffered much as I did. He said something I did not catch.

'What did you say?' I asked.

'Water, water,' he croaked, 'water, roll-call.' Gesticulating, he tried to explain what he had in mind. At last the penny dropped. What he proposed was that he and I should creep downstairs into the yard. There stood the vats of tea ready for the evening and we would have a chance to quench our thirst. I liked the idea: the timing seemed just right, for most of the prisoners were still asleep. Besides, the thought that tonight Vacek might once again decide to tip the tea into the gully-drain was an added incentive to go ahead with Maurice's daring plan. The anticipation of assuaging my raging thirst let me forget my fear of being caught. Noiselessly we climbed down from our bunks and tiptoed to the half-open door. Maurice peered to the right and to the left, then he made a sign for me to follow him. Step by step, cautiously and quiet as mice we felt our way down the stone stairs. In the yard all was as silent as the grave. To the right my glance skimmed over the black wall, the wall of execution. I did not look at the gallows in the corner. My attention was drawn to the left where two wooden vats brimful of tea were standing side by side. Crazed with thirst we pounced. For one brief moment I caught sight of my gaunt and distorted face reflected on the surface of the dark liquid, and I was shocked – but only for the fraction of a second. Bent over the rim of the vat I first carefully moistened my lips, then I drank, greedily, slowly, rapturously, the tepid refreshing tea. I came up for air briefly, then I propped my hands on the rim and drank and drank.

Suddenly I felt my neck gripped as in a vice : someone had taken hold of me and was forcing my head into the vat. I tried to wriggle out of the iron grasp. In vain. Desperately I opened my mouth to gasp for air, but my head had been forced well down and the tea penetrated into my lungs. My head was throbbing, I choked : someone was trying to drown me like a rat. Then I passed out. When I came to I was lying on the ground, my legs aching, my head bursting with pain, and a strange crackling noise in my ears. From far away I heard a voice bawling : 'Quick! Get up! You fucking bolshevik Yids! Get cracking! At the double!' There was a fierce stabbing pain every time I tried to open my eyes. Gradually I managed to distinguish the vague outlines of three figures. When I could focus more clearly, they turned out to be Schlage, Vacek, and a stocky SS leader whom I had not seen before, but whom I was to meet again that night. Obviously they had been waiting for us to come round. No doubt in their view half-drowning us was letting us off far too lightly for the heinous crime we had committed : clearly much worse was to come.

I stood up with difficulty. The sight of Maurice who was lying on the floor, deathly pale and still unconscious, frightened me. But after a while he, too, regained consciousness and rose to his feet. Vacek led us into the building. Opposite the *Blockführer*'s* room he made us stand with our faces to the wall. My legs felt wobbly and I was afraid. While we were standing there waiting my imagination ran riot : what were they going to do to us ? Perhaps they would wait until we had regained our strength and then put us through the *sport* routine. I imagined I could hear the commands 'Lie down! Up, at the double! Look lively! Run! Lie down!' fired at us

9

like bullets from a machine-gun, and just as lethal. Gingerly I shifted the weight of my body from one leg to the other in order to give some relief to my aching limbs. But I did not dare turn round. The slightest noise terrified me: for at any moment our tormentors might return. Time seemed to stand still, every second was an eternity. In my head my thoughts were racing round and round. The whole fearful catalogue of tortures by means of which prisoners were despatched passed before my mind's eye: would we get twenty-five strokes on the bare buttocks; or have our hands tied behind our backs and then be suspended by them; or left to starve in a black hole, a cell without any light?; and then there was *sport* in the yard. Somehow the prospect of *sport* terrified me most of all. Perhaps I could manage to stand up 100 or even 150 times. But there would come the moment when I no longer had the strength to do so. And then Vacek would finish me off with his truncheon as he had those thirty-five this morning.

Chapter 2
Into the crematorium

In my terror I heard neither the ringing of the bell nor the door being unlocked. It was only when Schlage shouted: 'Get out of here, you fucking thieves!' that Maurice and I raced out into the yard where an SS guard was waiting for us. He hustled us to the main gate where he handed us over to two SS men who took us to the right behind the *Blockführer*'s room, their pistols at the ready. At any moment I expected a bullet through the base of my skull. Instead, from not very far off, I heard music. It was one of Schubert's songs, and it was, without doubt, being performed by a real live orchestra. I briefly put aside my sombre thoughts of dying for, I argued, that in a place where Schubert's Serenade was sung to the accompaniment of an orchestra, there must surely be room for a little humanity.

We had been running for about 100 metres, when a strange flat-roofed building loomed up before us. Behind it a round red-brick chimney rose up into the sky. Through a wooden gate the two guards led us into a yard which was separated from the outside world by a wall. To our right was the building we had seen, with an entrance in the middle. Above the door hung a wrought-iron lamp. Under it stood an SS man who, according to his insignia, was an *Unterscharführer**. He was still young, with sandy hair and a commanding presence, and I learned later that his name was Stark. In his hand he held a horsewhip. He greeted us with the words: 'Get inside, you scum!' Then, belabouring us with his whip, he drove us through the entrance into a passage with several doors which were painted pale blue. We were confused and did not know which way we were meant to go. 'Straight ahead, you shits!' Stark shouted, opening one of the doors. The damp stench of dead bodies and a cloud of stifling, biting smoke surged out towards us. Through the fumes I saw the vague outlines of huge ovens. We were in the cremation room of the Auschwitz crematorium. A few prisoners, the Star of David on their prison uniforms, were running about. As the glow of the flames broke through the smoke and fumes, I noticed two large openings: they were cast-iron incinerators. Prisoners were busy pushing a truck heaped with corpses up to them. Stark pulled open another door. Flogging Maurice and me, he hustled us into a larger room next door to the cremation plant.

We were met by the appalling sight of the dead bodies of men and women lying higgledy-piggledy among suit-cases and rucksacks. I was petrified with horror. For I did not know then where I was and what was going on. A violent blow accompanied by Stark yelling: 'Get a move on! Strip the stiffs!' galvanized me into action. Before me lay the corpse of a woman. With trembling hands and shaking all over I began to remove her stockings. It was the first time in my life that I had touched a dead body. She was not yet quite cold. As I pulled the stocking down her leg, it tore. Stark who had been watching, struck me again, bellowing: 'What the hell d'you think you're doing? Mind out, and get a move on! These things are to be used again!' To show us the correct way he began to remove the stockings from another female corpse. But he, too, did not manage to take them off without at least a small tear.

I was like one hypnotized and obeyed each order implicitly. Fear of more blows, the ghastly sight of piled-up corpses, the biting smoke, the humming of fans and the flickering of flames, the whole infernal chaos had paralysed my sense of orientation as well as my ability to think. It took some time before I began to realize that there were people lying there at my feet who had been killed only a short while before. But what I could not imagine was how so many people could have been killed at one time.

When Stark returned he ordered Maurice and myself to the cremation room. Handing each of us a long crow-bar and a heavy hammer he ordered us to remove the clinker from the grates of those ovens which were not then in use. Neither Maurice nor I had ever done any work like this before, so we did not know what we were supposed to do. Instead of hammering the crow-bars into the clinker on the grates we thrust them into the ash pit and damaged the fire-brick lining. When Stark discovered the damage we had done, he hustled us back into the room where the corpses were and fetched a prisoner called Fischl – later to become our foreman – who went on with cleaning the grates.

Maurice and I continued stripping corpses. Cautiously I began to look round. I noticed that there were some small greenish-blue crystals lying on the concrete floor at the back of the room. They were scattered beneath an opening in the ceiling. A large fan was installed up there, its blades humming as they revolved. It struck me that where the crystals were scattered on the floor there were no corpses, whereas in places further away, particularly near the door, they were piled high.

My stay in the camp had undermined my health. I was weakened by starvation, my feet were swollen and the soles raw from wearing rough wooden clogs. It was therefore not surprising that, with the constant rush and hurry, I longed for a moment of rest. I kept a watchful eye on Stark and waited for a chance to take a breather while he was not looking. My moment came when he went across to the cremation room. Out of the corner of my eye I noticed a half-open suit-case containing food. Pretending to be busy undressing a corpse with one hand, I ransacked the suit-case with the other. Keeping one eye on the door in case Stark returned suddenly I hastily grabbed a few triangles of cheese and a poppyseed cake. With my filthy, blood-stained fingers I broke off pieces of cake and devoured them ravenously. I had only just time to pocket a piece of bread when Stark returned. He clearly thought we were slacking and shouted at us to work faster. An hour later we had undressed about 100 corpses. There they lay, naked and ready to be cremated.

In another suit-case I found a round box of cheese and several boxes of matches with Slovakian labels. And as I looked a little more closely at the faces of the dead, I recoiled with horror when I discovered among them a girl who had been at school with me. Her name was Yolana Weis. In order to make quite sure I looked at her hand because Yolana's hand had been deformed since childhood. I had not been mistaken: this was Yolana. There was another dead body which I recognized. It was that of a woman who had been our neighbour in Sered, my home town. Most of the dead were dressed in civilian clothes, but there were a few wearing military uniforms. Two wide, red stripes on the back of their jackets and the letters SU in black showed them to be Soviet prisoners of war.

Meanwhile Fischl had finished cleaning the grates. Now all six ovens were working, and Stark ordered us to drag the naked corpses across the concrete floor to the ovens. There Fischl went from corpse to corpse, forcing their mouths open with an iron bar. When he found a gold tooth he pulled it out with a pair of pliers and flung it into a tin. Stripped and robbed of everything the dead were destined to become victims of the flames and to be turned into smoke and ashes. Final preparations were now in hand. Stark ordered the fans to be switched on. A button was pressed and they began to rotate. But as soon as Stark had checked that the fire was drawing well they were switched off again. At his order 'Shove'em in!' each one of us set to work doing the job he had been given earlier.

I now began to realize the dangerous position in which I found myself. At that moment I had only one chance to stay alive, even if only for a few hours or days. I had to convince Stark that I could do anything he expected from a crematorium worker. And thus I carried out all his orders like a robot.

Coming from the room where I had been undressing corpses into the cremation room, there were two ovens on the left and four on the right. A depression roughly 20 to 25 centimetres deep and 1 metre wide ran across the room and in this rails had been laid. This track was about 15 metres long. Leading off from the main track were six branch rails, each 4 metres long, going straight to the ovens. On the main track was a turn-table which enabled a truck to be moved onto the branch tracks. The cast-iron truck had a box-shaped superstructure made of sheet metal, with an overall height and width of just under 1 metre. It was about 80 centimetres long. An iron hand-rail went right across its entire width at the back. A loading platform made of strong sheet metal and not quite 2 metres long jutted out in the front; its side walls were 12 to 15 centimetres high. Open at the front, the platform was not quite as wide as the mouth of the oven so that it fitted easily into the muffle. On the platform there was also a box-shaped pusher made of sheet metal, higher than the side walls of the platform and rounded off at the top. It was about 50 centimetres deep, 30 to 40 centimetres high and could be moved back and forth quite easily. Before the truck was loaded, the pusher was moved to the back of the platform. To move the truck from one track to another one had to hold onto the turn-table to prevent the truck from jumping off the rails as it left the turn-table.

To begin with, the corpses were dragged close to the ovens. Then, with the help of the turn-table, the truck was brought up to a branch rail, and the front edge of the platform supported by a wooden prop to prevent the truck from tipping during loading. A prisoner then poured a bucket of water on the platform to stop it from becoming too hot inside the red-hot oven. Meanwhile two prisoners were busy lifting a corpse onto a board lying on the floor beside the platform. Then they lifted the board, tipping it sideways so that the corpse dropped on the platform. A prisoner standing on the other side checked that the body was in correct position.

When the truck was fully loaded two corpses were lying on either side facing the oven while a third was wedged between them feet first. Now the time had come to open the oven door. Immediately one was overcome by the fierce heat which rushed out. When the wooden prop had been removed, two men took hold of the front end of the platform on either side pulling it right up to the oven. Simultaneously two men pushed the truck from behind, thus forcing the platform into the oven. The two who had been doing the carrying in front, having meanwhile nipped back a few steps, now braced themselves against the hand-rail while giving the pusher a vigorous shove with one leg. In this way they helped complete the job of getting the corpses right inside the oven. As soon as the front part of the pusher was inside the oven, the truck with its platform was pulled back. In order to prevent the load of corpses from sliding out of the oven during this operation, a prisoner standing to one side thrust an iron fork into the oven pressing it against the corpses. While the platform – which had been more than three-quarters inside the oven – was being manoeuvred on its truck back onto the turn-table, the oven door was closed again.

During one such operation I was kneeling by the turn-table holding onto it with all my strength so that the truck might roll on smoothly. But, my hands being unsteady, I failed to set the turn-table exactly in line with the track which resulted in the empty truck jumping rails as it rattled back from the oven. I felt a sharp pain in the little finger of my right hand and saw that I was bleeding. This wound nearly frightened me out of my wits. I vaguely remembered being told about ptomaine poisoning as a child. Quickly I tore a piece out of my sweaty shirt and tried to bandage my wound. At that moment nothing else seemed to matter; my mind was completely preoccupied with the wound.

And then Stark appeared. He was annoyed about the derailed truck and began to hit me. I screamed with pain. Then, making one last and desperate effort, I jumped up and helped to put the truck back onto the track. Of one thing I was quite sure: any failure on my part to comply would have meant instant death.

When all six ovens were loaded, we returned to our job of stripping corpses. I worked with the greatest care, anxiously trying to prevent my wounded finger from coming into contact with a dead body. Stark was standing in the doorway from where he could observe both rooms. My wound continued to bleed and had already soaked through my emergency bandage. Thus it happened that a little blood spilled on an undergarment just as Stark was standing near me. He noticed it at once and, raising his horsewhip, he shouted at me: 'You there, go and poke the stiffs, and be quick about it!' Although I quite failed to grasp what precisely it was he wanted me to do, I ran instinctively into the cremation room where I looked round completely at a loss. And then I saw Fischl: he walked up to one of the ovens and, lifting a flap in the lower half of the oven door, he proceeded to poke about inside the oven with a long fork. 'Come on, grab hold of this,' he whispered, 'poke the fork in and rattle it about, it'll make them burn better. Quick, or he'll kill you.' I grabbed this devil's tool and used it as Fischl had shown me, poking about among the burning disintegrating corpses as though I was poking a coal fire with a poker.

The powers that be had allocated twenty minutes for the cremation of three corpses. It was Stark's duty to see to it that this time was strictly adhered to. All at once, while I busied myself with my ghoulish task, three prisoners started to scurry around crazily in front of the ovens. They had refused to go on working and were trying to dodge Stark's blows. In the end they flung themselves on the concrete floor and, crawling on their bellies before him, implored him for pity's sake to finish them off with a bullet. Stark drove them into the room where the corpses lay and ordered them to get on with their work. But once again they threw themselves on the floor: they were beyond caring. Stark went purple with rage. His hand clutching the horsewhip was raised to come down on them in yet another vicious blow when suddenly he stopped short and simply said venomously: 'Just you wait, you lazy bastards, you've got it coming to you!' Then without another word he returned to the cremation room where he could be heard issuing orders.

When all six ovens were working, Stark hustled us next door to strip more corpses while he stayed behind in the cremation room. Meanwhile, pretending all the time to be working hard, I was trying desperately to gather new strength. Among the dead bodies I discovered our three fellow prisoners. Although they were still breathing, they were lying quite still, all their physical energy and the spiritual will to live drained out of them. They had given up.

I, on the other hand, had not yet reached that point of despair. Of course, I had no illusions: I knew with certainty that a dreadful end awaited me. But I was not yet ready to capitulate. The more menacing death grew, the stronger grew my will to survive. My every thought, every fibre of my being, was concentrated on only one thing: to stay alive, one minute, one hour, one day, one week. But not to die. I was still young, after all. The memory of my parents, my family and my early youth in my home town had faded. I was obsessed and dominated by the determination that I must not die. The heap of dead bodies which I had seen and which I was made to help remove only served to strengthen my determination to do everything possible not to perish in the same way; not to have to lie under a heap of dead bodies; not to be pushed into the oven, prodded with an iron fork and, ultimately, changed into smoke and ashes. Anything but that! I only wanted one thing: to go on living. Sometime, somehow, there might be a chance to get out of here. But if I wanted to survive there was only one thing: I must submit and carry out every single order. It was only by adopting this attitude that a man was able to carry on his ghastly trade in the crematorium of Auschwitz.

By late afternoon the fire had reduced many of the dead bodies into ashes. Yet the bulk of them was still lying about because, with three corpses going into each oven at intervals of twenty minutes, it was impossible to cremate more than fifty-four in one hour. I calculated that it would take quite a time before all the dead were cremated. And what would happen to us then? I tried to push this unanswerable question to the back of my mind. Perhaps no decision would be taken until tomorrow. And today I was still alive. That was the main thing.

While the bodies were being cremated we prepared a further load for the ovens. Still there were only four of us. We were rushing around in double-quick time, each one of us having to do the work of two men. There was not a moment to pause to draw breath. Exhausted and stupefied by the constant rush we had forgotten to switch off one set of fans, simply because we no longer noticed their humming. They had fanned the flames to such an extent that because of the intense heat the fire-bricks in the chimney had become loose and fallen into the duct connecting the oven to the chimney. This meant that the flames no longer had a way out; fiery red tongues were licking out of the oven and in no time the cremation room was enveloped in a dense fog of sickly choking smoke. Stark was rushing around like a madman and finally dashed outside towards a wooden hut which housed the headquarters of the political department* in whose offices sat his superiors. Presently he returned accompanied by several SS men who showed us how to extinguish the fire. After attaching a hose to a tap we opened one of the ovens and attempted to douse the flames with a jet of water. As this hit the fire there was a sound of hissing and crackling as if a lump of ice had been thrown into a pan of boiling fat. The flames died down, but underneath the surface the fire continued to smoulder with greyish-black smoke belching out of the oven. From gaps in the doors of the remaining five ovens puffs of fumes and flames kept bursting forth every few seconds. Stark was dashing about in great agitation, shouting at us to fetch water in buckets. Then we tore open the doors of the remaining five ovens. Amid blows, threats and a great deal of shouting on the part of the SS men we raced to the ovens with buckets of water from the tap and emptied them onto the grates. Blood-stained from blows we struggled with the flames for another half hour until at long last the fire-brigade, manned by prisoners, arrived. They directed their hose first at the chimney and the flat roof of the crematorium.

Stark was still scurrying around nervously. Of all the SS men he was the one most agitated. Perhaps he feared that he would be held responsible for the blaze. Suddenly I heard some shots in the next room where the three prisoners who had refused to go on working were lying on the floor. Some time later I looked through the half-open door and saw that they had been shot in the head. Obviously it was thought that these three were responsible for the fire, because the four of us on our own had been unable to cope with the work.

There was now a distinctly strange atmosphere. Nobody shouted any longer, nobody aimed blows at us. Like condemned criminals waiting for their execution we sat in a corner of the cremation chamber without anybody taking any notice of us. Night was falling. Electric bulbs gleamed feebly through the misty grey of the evening, like candles in the churchyard on All Soul's Day. The black wrought-iron lantern over the entrance to the crematorium spread its dim light, tracing the contours of the vine leaves, the grey wall and the heavy door. An unsuspecting passer-by might have assumed the comfort of a cosy home behind this pleasant façade. Nobody would have believed that this door was the entrance gate to hell. Neither, I daresay, did the three fellow prisoners who had come to join us guess where this romantic gate was to lead them. They had been brought here by the SS guard, as had we that afternoon, to replace the three prisoners whom Stark had shot. I allowed myself to be a little more hopeful.

Late that night a tarpaulin-covered lorry backed into the crematorium yard. Some time later a group of SS leaders appeared in the yard. *Unterscharführer* Stark and his henchmen stood to attention, smartly raised their right arm and shouted a brisk '*Heil Hitler!*'. After a brief report we were ordered to load on the truck the remaining corpses which had by now been stripped of their clothes.

Maurice and I dragged the dead bodies outside across the slippery concrete floor of the crematorium. Then we grabbed them by their hands and feet and flung them on the truck where two prisoners stacked them like logs, one on top of the other. All this took place at break-neck speed with the SS men shouting at us to work faster, and faster still. The new men were utterly dazed and shrank from touching the slippery corpses. Often they lost hold of the damp hands, arms, legs and trunks and let the dead bodies fall to the ground. The SS men reacted with renewed beatings. When two of the newcomers fell down under the blows abuse was heaped on them: 'If you stupid swine bust the ovens, we'll have to find other ways of doing things. Up there with those stiffs, and get the hell on with it or I'll have your balls off!' The most loud-mouthed and evil-tongued of them all, his voice hoarse and thick like an alcoholic's, was the short SS leader whom I had encountered that afternoon by the tea vats. There he was, with legs apart, arms akimbo, his body slightly bent forward, watching us at work. Now and then he turned to the SS leaders and deputy leaders by his side and explained something to them, obviously very full of himself. Later we learned that this was *SS-*

*Hauptsturmführer** Hans Aumeier who was in charge of the main camp. Beside him was the chief of the Gestapo's political department, *SS-Untersturmführer** Max Grabner.

Meanwhile the truck had been piled to overflowing with corpses. The tail-board was raised and fastened and the tarpaulin firmly secured all round to make quite sure that nothing betrayed its ghastly load. Thus camouflaged the truck left the crematorium and was parked by the roadside not far from the SS hospital.

Shortly before midnight we had finished loading the fourth and last truck. We squeezed ourselves into a small space at the back, in between the corpses, leaning against them as against a wall, without giving them the least thought. Before we left, an SS man distributed bread rations. Our hands were filthy with blood and excrement, but we did not care: hunger and starvation had taught us to appreciate a hunk of bread. The mere sight of it was enough to make us forget all else. I broke off small pieces, holding them in my mouth until they were soaked with saliva. Then I chewed them slowly and deliberately as though savouring a great delicacy. I did not notice that the truck had begun to move, and it was only when intermittent shafts of light started to penetrate our darkness that I realized we were on our way. Curiously I lifted a corner of the tarpaulin. The light came from the headlamps of a car which was following us. Doubtless it was to keep an eye on us in case we tried to escape under cover of darkness. They had overestimated our store of energy; we were so weak and dejected that at that moment no one was even thinking of flight.

Through a chink between the tail-board and the tarpaulin I noticed that we were passing through a small town. Now and then a solitary pedestrian walked the nocturnal roads. Presumably we were driving through Auschwitz. The sound of our engines echoed in the empty streets. When the ghostly convoy had passed the last houses the road began to climb slightly as we crossed a railway line. Judging from the jolts and bumps we were now going down a country lane. I turned round and noticed to my horror that the corpses behind us had started to move. Rocked and jolted by the journey over uneven terrain, our gruesome cargo had begun to sway. It seemed as though the dead had come to life again. When the driver suddenly slammed on the brakes as he went round a bend the top layer of bodies slid into the rear part of the cargo space and came down on top of us. Dozens of corpses, stiff as boards, pinned us down. I lay on my stomach on the floor of the truck; any attempt to free myself was quite futile. Every jolt increased the pressure and I could scarcely breathe. I shouted for help, but my voice was drowned by the noise of the engine and the creaking of the truck body. My six companions fared no better. It was as though all these slippery, rigid bodies were determined to bury us beneath them and take us with them to their final doom.

At long last the truck stopped. An SS man was shouting: 'Come on, come on! Didn't you hear? Get down! Come along! Out! Get a move on!' As far as the corpses were concerned these threats left them, literally, cold; and we could not make ourselves heard. Only when the headlamps of the car behind us cast their light on the back of our truck, did the SS men have an inkling of what had happened. After they had let down the tail-board and removed several corpses we were able to free ourselves. I was aching all over: I felt as though I had fractured every single bone in my body. My companions, too, were groaning. We sat on the ground gasping for air. A few steps away stood the four trucks loaded to bursting point, as well as an ambulance marked on all sides with red crosses. Headlights illuminated a large area with a deep oval-shaped pit in the middle. At its bottom a pool of water had formed in which the moon was mirrored. Round the edge of the pit loose and obviously freshly dug clay had been heaped. From the conversation among the SS men near by I gathered that, unexpectedly, ground-water had seeped through into the pit, and now they did not seem quite sure whether this pit was suitable for the purpose for which it had been dug. They made a detailed inspection of the clay round the edge and one of them was let down into the pit on the end of a rope. When he came up, he reported on the height of the ground-water and they went into another huddle trying to decide what to do.

At this point my tiredness got the better of my curiosity and I fell asleep lying on the ground. I was awoken by the sound of cars approaching. A group of SS leaders, with *Lagerführer** Aumeier and Gestapo chief Grabner at the head, climbed out. They walked up to the pit, examining and looking at it from every angle, after which they conferred for a while. Then we were ordered to start throwing the corpses into the pit. First two prisoners threw them down from the truck; then our three companions from France dragged them to the edge of the pit where Maurice and I were standing ready. Grabbing the corpses by their hands and feet we pitched them as far as we could towards the middle of the pit.

There was a splash of water as they fell, then they sank to the shallow bottom. Gradually our strength began to fail and we barely managed to dispose of the last few corpses from the first truck. When the SS men noticed that we were fairly whacked they ordered the French prisoners to relieve us.

It was almost dawn when we returned to camp. Everybody was still asleep. Hundreds of light-bulbs fastened to the concrete poles of the barbed-wire fence bordered the camp road, which was quite empty. Only the clip-clop of our wooden clogs echoed through the ghostly silence. Surrounding us were endless parallel rows of barbed wire with their warning notices 'Caution – Danger' underneath a skull and cross-bones; pointing at us were the mouths of machine-guns mounted on the watch-towers; the place we were bound for was one of the desolate red-brick buildings which housed the camp prisoners. It was enough to plunge anyone into a state of utter hopelessness and boundless despair. That was why many people, once they realized their situation, chose to put an end to their misery. This morning as we were returning to camp we saw several dead bodies lying in the 'forbidden zone', or 'death strip', as the area along the high-tension wire fences was called in concentration camp slang. 'He has gone to the wire', was camp slang for a prisoner who had been released from his sufferings either by an electric shock or by a burst from a machine-gun before he could reach the fence.

The entrance door to Block 11 was locked. One of the guards rang the bell: *Oberscharführer* Plagge unlocked the door and let us in. The nocturnal stillness was disturbed only by the rattling of his keys as he led us down to the labyrinth of prison cells in the cellar. The lock creaked as Plagge unlocked the iron-barred door through which we went into the centre corridor. At once we were met by a choking stench. In the dim light the whitewashed walls stood out against the black floor. There was neither window nor ventilation in the cell, three paces long, three paces wide, into which Plagge hustled us. The cell door was locked and at once the light went out. We were dead tired and fell asleep as soon as we were stretched out on the floor. At last the end of this long and eventful day had come.

When I awoke I guessed that it must be morning outside. I could only deduce this from the voices I could hear, for no light, not the smallest shaft, could have found its way into our cell, and we could not tell what time it was. In this state of isolation, of being totally cut off from the outside world, camp life seemed a positive oasis of freedom to me.

We urinated on the cell floor like animals in a shed, for in the complete darkness nobody noticed that by the door stood a wooden-lidded bucket. My body still ached all over and the slightest movement was agony. In addition I was tormented by an intolerable thirst.

The rattling of keys, the opening of iron-barred gates, the unlocking of cell doors, the steps of prison guards, all these sounds aroused in the prisoners locked in their cells a feeling of almost unbearable tension. For no one knew what the unlocking of his cell might signify for him. Perhaps he had been granted the longed-for return to the 'freedom of the camp'. On the other hand it could well be that they would lead him out into the yard, stand him against the black wall and finish him off with a bullet in the nape of his neck. Or worse still, it could mean an interrogation in the political department of the Gestapo which almost invariably included prolonged and cruel torture.

As for us, we registered any sign of life in the corridor outside our cell as a good omen. And yet we waited in vain for somebody to let us out. They simply left us in uncertainty, in absolute darkness, worse than cattle. At last, after an interminable wait, the light was switched on. The door was unlocked, Schlage appeared and hustled us into the corridor where an SS man was waiting for us. He took us to the main gate. Clearly it was already midday, for the barrack orderlies were coming out of the kitchen building carrying cauldrons of turnip soup on long poles. The sun shone on the camp street which was teeming with prisoners. Even though they lived behind barbed wire they seemed to me to be free, and I envied them. A few turned round as though they meant to talk to us, but turned away as soon as they noticed our hands and faces encrusted with blood and the mud on our clogs. Most of them went past without noticing us. Their stomachs were rumbling and they were interested only in the impending ritual of the ladling out of soup.

A green ambulance was waiting for us outside the gate. We climbed in and found awaiting us a cauldron of steaming soup. There were some twenty-five litres, about 3 litres for each of us. After we had filled ourselves up with thin turnip soup we looked out of the barred window of the ambulance. The sun was high in the sky and shone over a flat and barren landscape; there was neither tree nor bush to be seen. Our journey took us past moors and marshy meadowland, here and there streaked with yellow or red clayey soil. This desolate wasteland was all round us wherever we turned. But far in the distance the silhouette of the Beskidy hills could just be made out. To me it seemed unreal that beyond, only a few hours' train journey away, lay Sered, my home town. There I had spent the first twenty years of my young life, until a little more than a month ago when I was deported to Auschwitz. Even this brief period of time seemed like eternity to me. The ambulance stopped. The door was pulled open by an SS man who ordered us to get out. We sat on the ground while the SS men stood round us. Next to a heap of clay near by a power pump was putt-putting away. Water was pouring from several hoses onto the surrounding fields. Behind the mound of clay we could not fail to recognize the pit into which we had thrown corpses during the previous night.

We looked at each other with fear in our eyes. SS men in thigh-high gum-boots were fiddling about with the pumps. They were tightening gaskets and laying hoses while others were standing on the mound of clay peering over the edge into the pit in order to watch the water level at the bottom. They might have been firemen or fishermen, busy draining a pond. I was sure that we must be prepared for the worst as soon as the draining operations had been completed. There was every likelihood that we might wind up as the top layer in the pit.

Once again I was seized by a feeling of uncontrollable fear, and there was nothing I could do about it. I tried to recall exemplary men and women down the centuries who were put to death. I remembered that we must all die. Death, I told myself, was, after all, part of our lives and we would have to face it sooner or later. Needless to say these considerations were quite futile and failed lamentably either to stifle or to dismiss my fears.

Armed SS men now led us to the pit. In broad daylight everything looked quite different. The 250 or so dead bodies did not even half-fill the pit. Their staring eyeballs protruded from their sockets, their swollen lips seemed to be covered with a bluey-red membrane. We were fascinated by this horrible manifestation of death and somehow even attracted, as though we were a part of it. But before we had time to take in this picture in all its gruesomeness, there was a hail of blows accompanied by shouts of 'Come on, you! Get down there, you shit! Get going! Get those stiffs in a heap, right in the middle of the pit!' Driven on by blows we leapt over the excavated clay into the pit, right among the corpses. I sank down in sticky, slimy mud, and after a few steps my clogs stuck fast. While we were trying to carry out their commands, the SS men stood round the rim of the pit constantly threatening and exhorting us. Some were waving their loaded pistols to lend more emphasis to their threats. I waded through the sludge to where a dead woman was lying at the edge. But when I tried to drag her towards the middle, her slippery hand slid out of mine: I stumbled and fell, face down, into the mud. With great effort I managed to get up again. My lips were tightly pressed together. I wiped my eyes and slowly opened my dirt-encrusted eyelids. My companions had not fared any better: they, too, were covered from head to foot in mud and slime.

After some delay two SS men were lowered into the pit on ropes while Aumeier, Schwarzhuber and Gestapo chief Grabner were running about like startled chickens. They conferred together, waved their hands about and shouted at us: 'If you don't get this job done, you Yids, you'll be sorry!'

The dead no longer cared where they lay, on top or underneath, at the edge or in the middle of the pit; nor did they mind that we were in trouble because of them as we tried desperately to fling their slippery bodies into this abyss of death.

The water in the pit began to rise again. The mud, doughy to begin with, now turned into a thin mush which made our work even harder. Two of the prisoners could not go on. Completely exhausted they lay at the edge of the pit trying to catch their breath and regain their strength. The face of one was encrusted with grey mud. Underneath one could still make out a black eye patch which covered an empty socket. A young student from Paris who had slipped and swallowed a lot of water was lying on the other side of the pit coughing and spluttering. The SS men were shouting in an attempt to get the two on their feet again. 'Come on, come on, quick, quick! Get up! You bastards! Get on with it!' But the two no longer responded, they had ceased to care. Aumeier who had been watching from a distance yelled: 'For heaven's sake, finish the bastards off!' His underlings drew their pistols. After two well-aimed shots in the head the two bodies slowly slumped. Trickles of blood appeared in the ground-water at the bottom of the pit. Now there were only five of us left, still lugging bodies into the centre of the pit where they formed some kind of pyramid which rose from the muddy water like an island.

Several hours later, our work finished, we climbed out. Looking down we beheld hundreds of arms, legs, lifeless faces and bodies intertwined in hideous confusion. We plunged our bare hands into a vat of chlorinated lime and sprinkled it on top of the corpses in the pit. The wind blew the powder into our faces so that we could scarcely keep our burning eyes open. But we dared not stop. One moment's pause would have meant certain death, so much was clear to everyone listening to the SS men's hysterical yelling. Fortunately the wind dropped. The white dust on top of the corpses had turned grey. The biting smell of chlorine mingled with the odour of decomposition. Then we began to shovel clay into the pit in order to make invisible the pyramid of dead bodies. We had to work with insane speed, in our ears the constant, never-ending threats and shouts of the SS men who were anxious to cover all traces of their crimes as quickly as possible. For them we were not working fast enough. As Aumeier, their boss, remarked succinctly: 'It's quite obvious that none of you Yids has ever done a proper job of work. But now there'll be no more haggling for any of you.' Even this threat had no effect, for we were far too exhausted. My heart sank when I thought of how much there was left for us to fill up. The bodies could no longer be seen because they were covered with a thin layer of soil. Mercifully the grave-diggers in uniform seemed to have had enough for one day. They prepared to depart, and another group of armed SS men took up guard round the mass grave.

Soaked to the skin, barefoot and covered from head to foot in mud and blood we climbed into the ambulance. The emblem of the International Red Cross seemed a symbol of grotesque mockery: we were convinced that there was no power on earth which could put an end to this diabolical nightmare. After what we had gone through that day the spark of life which still glimmered within us had dimmed.

Nothing could be seen through the windows of the ambulance as it drove through the dusk. Exhausted I lay down on the floor of the vehicle. I closed my eyes. Midway between sleeping and waking I was back at Sered on Waag. I saw again the lean *Kommandant* of the Slovak Hlinka Guards good-naturedly saying to us: 'When you get to your new homes in the East, you'll be able to build a new life for yourselves. There's no need to be afraid. *We* are treating you humanely, and it'll be the same when you get there. Each one of you will do what he can. The shoemaker will make shoes, the tailor suits and dresses, and the doctors look after the sick. What's more, you'll be among your own people! Anyone who is healthy and not afraid of work will do well out there. Every now and then we'll come and visit you, to look after things and see how you're getting on.' Following this speech we had climbed into the goods waggons which were standing ready in the siding at Sered station. The leader of the Hlinka Guards – a kind of Slovak SS – had waved us a jolly good-bye and wished us *bon voyage*.

The ambulance stopping outside the camp gate, which bore the inscription 'Work liberates', jolted me back into harsh reality. Once more we were escorted by guards through the gate and along the camp street which ran between the two-storey red-brick prison blocks. We halted outside Block 11. *Oberscharführer* Engelschall who happened to be on duty hustled us back into our dark cell. On the floor lay seven portions of bread and cheese, but there were only three portions of tea in red-enamelled tin bowls. When Engelschall locked our cell door he left the light on, and at that moment he seemed to us more human than any of his colleagues, and even quite decent, for at least we could now eat properly. To begin with we wolfed down the bread and cheese. But when it came to drinking the tea, there were problems. There were five of us, but only three bowls of tea. Fischl, who was the strongest and most forceful, lifted one of the bowls and indicated with his finger the level down to which each of us was allowed to drink. As the youngest I was given what was left in each bowl. When we had finished the tea there were still two portions of bread, meant for the two French prisoners, untouched on the floor. Painstakingly Fischl divided them into five equal parts which he distributed among us. While we were devouring our extra rations, Fischl began muttering a prayer. Looking up at the low ceiling as though he could see heaven there, he rocked back and forth, turning to the right and to the left and invoking God. From the few words I managed to catch I gathered that he was reciting the Kaddish, the prayer for the dead. Suddenly, as though coming out of a trance, he stared at us absent-mindedly. When he saw that we were still busy chewing while he was at prayer, he belaboured us with his fists shouting in Yiddish: 'You sons of bitches, all you can do is gobble, but you can't be bothered to pray for the dead whose bread you're gobbling.' Then, lifting his bloodshot eyes to heaven and overcome by emotion, he finished his prayer with the words: 'May He who maketh peace in his high heavens, grant peace unto us and unto all Israel. And say ye, amen.'

Fischl was our foreman, a thick-set, brawny man. When he had finished his prayers he looked more peaceable. There were tears in his eyes. A little later he said quietly: 'Man differs from animals in that he believes in God.' That day his last words before he settled down to sleep, spoken in Yiddish, were: 'It's prayer which makes you a human being. Good night to you, fellow Jews!'

We lay on the floor in our filthy uniforms and were fast asleep in an instant. It was the end of another hard day. Next morning when Engelschall unlocked the door we were lying there snoring, like mud-encrusted hippos. We must have been a shocking sight, for Engelschall barked at us: 'Get into the wash-room, you pigs!' Sleepily we tottered out into the corridor from where he led us up to the wash-room on the groundfloor. On the way I had a glimpse of the *sports ground* through a window: it was empty and deserted.

It was rather cold in the wash-room. But for once there was actually water running from the taps, a rare chance to quench one's thirst. I turned on the tap and drank my fill. Then we undressed, laid our filthy clothes on the wet concrete floor and attempted to remove the crust of filth and mud from our bodies. We were issued with a new striped prison uniform and a fresh shirt. Then we returned to the underworld, but not this time to our dungeon but to cell 13 where there was some daylight. The window through which this precious daylight came gave out onto the yard where executions took place. However, it was surrounded by walls on all sides so that light could penetrate only from above; it was impossible to look out. We lay down on the floor but sleep would not come. We wondered what might be the meaning of the clean uniforms and the daylight.

Fischl ascribed this obvious turn for the better to his prayers and to the Lord. 'The Lord will help! Time to pray, lads!' With these words he rose and, turning his face to the window, he began in a low voice to say the morning prayer. As he did not possess the Tephillim, the leather straps without which no orthodox Jew may recite this particular prayer, he mimed the ritual of putting them round his hands and forehead with a deftness which I had vainly tried to acquire long ago when our rabbi was preparing me for my barmitzvah*. While he was praying he gave us a signal when it was time for us to rise. Every time he nodded his head after a certain passage, we responded by saying 'Amen'. To me it seemed sheer madness to pray in Auschwitz, and absurd to believe in God in this place. In any other situation and in any other place I should not have taken Fischl seriously. But here, on the border-line between life and death, we obediently followed his example, possibly because we had nothing else left or because we felt strengthened by his faith.

Our life of isolation continued. For, although we did not realize this at first, we had become privy to a secret and were no longer allowed to come into contact with other prisoners or with SS men not in the know. That was why we no longer attended roll-call. We were accounted for on a special list of prisoners on which we were referred to only by our cell number. During the next few days our cell door was opened three times a day at meal times. Nobody took us to work; it was as if we had been forgotten. And yet there was plenty of activity in the cellar of Block 11. This day the iron door and barred gate of the prison clanked open once again. From the conversations outside we gathered that a group of SS men had arrived. They unlocked one cell after another, and each time we heard a prisoner shout 'Attention!' in great agitation. Among the voices I recognized the hoarse croaking of the alcoholic Aumeier and brisk interjections by Grabner, chief of the camp Gestapo.

As they went from cell to cell the duty officer accompanying them explained the reason for each prisoner's detention. Then they conferred briefly and announced their verdict, which in most cases was a terse 'Come on, outside!' With these three words, the equivalent of a court-martial, they selected the prisoners who were to die. When they arrived in the cell next to ours we, too, were overcome by fear and agitation. But they went past our cell and entered the next one. The selection of prisoners for execution lasted an hour. The sequel took place at the black wall of death. Although unable to look out into the yard, we could hear the sound of desperate wailing and lamenting, and of God being invoked; but now and then there were also shouts in Polish or Russian, like 'Long live free Poland!' or 'Long live Stalin!' Aumeier clearly disliked such scenes. To make himself understood by his victims, he used the only word of their mother tongue he had managed to pick up. While he croaked '*Szybko, Szybko*' (faster, faster), they were despatched into the next world with brisk efficiency. Rigid with terror we sat on the floor of our cell listening to the peculiar noise of the silenced small-bore rifles. Thus we were, so to speak, present at the execution acoustically. If every shot denoted one prisoner killed, then more than a hundred were killed that day. Once again death had reaped a rich harvest by the black wall. When it was all over, there was deathly silence, interrupted only by the shout: 'Ration carriers, fall out!' Some time later soup was brought to us. We ate our meal and while thus occupied forgot everything else.

We had spent several days idle in our cell when after evening roll-call – at which, of course, we had not been present – the door was suddenly opened. Outside in the corridor stood Stark, beside him a prisoner whom we did not know. Obviously he was to take the place of the two who had been shot in the pit. After we had left the block, Stark made us run towards the main gate and from there straight to the crematorium yard. There we were made to stand by the wall beside the barred window of the cremation room. Stark swore us to secrecy, threatening us with dire punishment in case we spoke to anybody who came here. With a wink he indicated to Fischl that he held him responsible for the strict compliance with this command. Obediently Fischl replied: 'Yes, *Herr Unterscharführer!*'

Stark – the name means 'strong' in English – did credit to his name. He was tall and well built and had sandy hair. His body was broad and strong and his legs sturdy and muscular: he was a healthy young man in his prime. His worst fault was his violent temper. When he blew his top – often for quite trivial reasons – it was best to make oneself scarce; otherwise things might turn very nasty indeed.

We prisoners and Stark were worlds apart. For us he seemed to have no human feelings whatever. We only knew him as one who gave his commands brusquely, insulted, abused and threatened us continually, goaded us to work, and beat us mercilessly. To his superiors he was assiduous and subservient. I often wondered how it was possible for this young man, scarcely older than myself, to be so cruel, so brutal, harbouring so unfathomable a hatred of the Jews. I doubted whether he had actually ever come into close contact with Jews before he came to Auschwitz. He was no doubt a victim of that Nazi propaganda which put the blame for any misfortune, including the war, on the Jews. How was it possible, I often asked myself, for a young man of average intelligence and normal personality to carry out the unspeakable atrocities demanded of him in the belief that thereby he was doing his patriotic duty, without ever realizing that he was being used as a tool by perverted political dictators?

All traces of the horror of the last few days had been removed. The very cobblestones in the yard had been hosed clean of blood and were sparkling. Behind the higher outer concrete wall, near the SS motor transport pool, a giant tree with wide-spread branches had begun to break into leaf. This day it, and we, were to witness an event to which Himmler, or perhaps even the Führer in person, had given the name of *Geheime Reichssache*, Secret Matter of the Reich.

There was a great hustle and bustle in the yard. First to appear were Quackernack, Stark, Kirschner, Dylewski and Palitzsch, all carrying truncheons. After them came the camp élite, Aumeier, Grabner and *Untersturmführer* Hössler, as well as another SS leader whom I did not know and who wore on his arm the emblem of the medical profession.

We had not been waiting long when a large number of people began to stream through the open gate, the majority of them dressed in dark clothes. On the right side at chest height they all wore the yellow Star of David. By and by the entire yard became crowded with these people who were talking to each other in Polish or Yiddish. Most were middle-aged, but there was a sprinkling of old men and women and also of children among them. They were rather out of breath as if they had been made to run all the way. Last to arrive was a group of aged women who had been unable to keep up with the younger people and who came staggering in on the point of complete exhaustion. Once the stragglers were inside the gate was shut.

The uniformed executioners now stepped in front of the waiting apprehensive crowd of several hundred. As though at a signal they began to harangue them, waving their truncheons about and ordering them to take their clothes off at once. The people were dazed with fear. Clearly they suspected that something dreadful was to befall them, but they could see no reason why they ought to undress out here in the yard, women in front of men and vice versa. However, the SS men, anxious to give them no time to think, kept shouting: 'Come on, come on! Get undressed! Get a move on! Come on! Come on! Get undressed!' At last I tumbled to what was going on. One of the SS men must have had the bright idea that it was more expedient to send these people to their doom naked. For then the irksome task of undressing them after their death would be avoided. Besides, if they undressed while still alive, their clothes would not be torn because they would think that they would need them again. Today this new procedure was to be tried out for the first time.

However, it did not quite work out according to plan. In the frightened and embarrassed faces of the men and women assembled in the yard there was fear and mistrust. Although unaware of what awaited them, they sensed the seriousness and danger of their situation. Most of the men reacted to the threats and shouts by slowly beginning to undo the collars of their shirts, while the women bent down and, greatly embarrassed, undid their shoe-laces. All this took a very long time: it was not at all the efficient operation the SS men had envisaged.

In a corner next to the gate I noticed a young woman and her child. Her lips tightly pressed together looked like a scar. She gazed at her small daughter then, stroking her, she slowly undressed her. Older children, as alarmed as their parents, began slowly to take off their clothes.

Meanwhile the representatives of the SS hierarchy stood on the earthworks which had been thrown up on the roof of the crematorium. From there they had a bird's eye view of what was going on. At first they did not intervene, leaving everything to their minions. But the alarm and disquiet of the people grew apace as did their fear of the danger they could sense: they were taking off their clothes with great deliberation in order to gain time.

These people came from the ghetto of Sosnovits only a few kilometres away. No doubt rumours about the camp at Auschwitz had reached them; no doubt they had wondered whether these were merely rumours or whether there might not be some truth in the tales that were going round. The brutal conduct of the SS surpassed their worst fears. They felt instinctively that they were in great danger and began to talk among themselves. In the yard there was a humming as in a beehive. Once it dawned on the SS men that their brilliant plan of deception was in jeopardy they flung themselves wildly into the crowd, wielding their truncheons indiscriminately and yelling: 'Come on, come on! Get undressed! Faster, faster!' The effect was startling. The people seemed to wake up from an oppressive sleep. The men who, up till then, had only undone a few buttons of collar and shirt, hastily took off their jackets, trousers and shoes. Many women were dashing about helplessly, seeking refuge with their husbands; frightened children were clinging more tightly to their mothers. The brutal action of the SS men had completely unnerved the people. They were confused, frightened, unable to communicate with each other and incapable of thinking. As the SS men persisted in their rampaging, the crowd was seized by panic. Even their passive resistance was now broken and they did what was being beaten into them again and again: 'Come on! Get undressed! Come on! Faster! Get a move on!' Men, women and children were now tearing their clothes off, helping each other to dodge the blows, and in no time at all they were all standing there naked, each with a small heap of clothes piled in front of them.

We, too, were horrified and shaking all over. Never before had I experienced anything so dreadful. Even Fischl, our god-fearing giant, was trembling, but he still had enough strength and faith for a prayer and he muttered the Shema, the Jewish equivalent of the Lord's Prayer. When he realized that his devout murmuring might attract the attention of the SS men, he fell silent. Though almost indispensable as a strong and dutiful robot, they might not have shown much appreciation for his religious fervour.

Once again I watched the young mother in the corner by the gate. Carrying her child on her arm she, too, was now undressed. She was not ashamed of her nakedness, but the premonition that perhaps she had undressed her child and herself for the last time put her into a state of helpless submission to God's will.

Two of the SS men took up positions on either side of the entrance door. Shouting and wielding their truncheons, like beaters at a hunt, the remaining SS men chased the naked men, women and children into the large room inside the crematorium. All that was left in the yard were the pathetic heaps of clothing which we had to gather together to clear the yard for the second half of the transport. We removed suit-cases, rucksacks, clothes and shoes and piled them higgledy-piggledy in a great heap in a corner. Then we covered everything with a large tarpaulin.

When we had finished, a new batch of several hundred people poured into the empty yard. The prelude to death was repeated with equal brutality and with the same ending. Finally there were about 600 desperate people crammed into the crematorium. A few SS men were leaving the building and the last one locked the entrance door from the outside. Before long the increasing sound of coughing, screaming and shouting for help could be heard from behind the door. I was unable to make out individual words, for the shouts were drowned by knocking and banging against the door, intermingled with sobbing and crying. After some time the noise grew weaker, the screams stopped. Only now and then there was a moan, a rattle, or the sound of muffled knocking against the door. But soon even that ceased and in the sudden silence each one of us felt the horror of this terrible mass death.

Once everything was quiet inside the crematorium, *Unterscharführer* Teuer, followed by Stark, appeared on the flat roof. Both had gas-masks dangling round their necks. They put down oblong boxes which looked like food tins; each tin was labelled with a death's head and marked *Poison!* What had been just a terrible notion, a suspicion, was now a certainty: the people inside the crematorium had been killed with poison gas.

When the SS men had gone, Stark ordered us to sort the clothes and to search them for money and valuables. He was particularly keen on the latter. The yard was dimly lit by the one lantern over the entrance. So we did only a very rough and ready kind of sorting. The objects which people had concealed in their pockets and shoes were proof of the fact that not one of them had expected death to await them at his journey's end.

We were ordered to place the valuables into separate boxes, foreign currency into one, watches into another, gold and jewellery into a third. Clothing, shoes and underwear were sorted into different heaps. There were separate heaps of knives, spectacles, bottles, medicines, and dolls which their little owners had left behind for ever. There was one large mound of prayer-books and velvet bags containing the Tephillim or phylacteries. Fischl seemed particularly interested in this collection; and during a moment when he was unobserved he managed to slip a Tephillim bag under his jacket. We piled the sorted objects on a trolley and took them to the camp's clothing stores. As I turned round, I saw Stark climbing across the sloping earth bank onto the roof. Soon afterwards the sound of the fan starting up could be heard.

It was late at night when we were locked into cell 13. Once again the light was left on for a while so that we could eat. Today we did not ravenously attack our rations, but instead pulled out from under shirts and jackets and from out of pockets stuff we had *organized**. One after the other we laid bread, sugar, saccharine, tobacco and other goodies in front of our foreman.

Fischl examined everything carefully. Then he divided the booty into seven scrupulously equal parts. In spite of what had happened today, Fischl appeared to be the most satisfied among us. The Lord Adonai had hearkened to him: now he owned a prayer-book in Hebrew and a set of Tephillim. Early next morning he went through the ritual of putting on the phylacteries – this time there was no need for him to mime the action – before saying his morning prayers. He prayed so fervently and humbly that God – if He existed – must surely have heard his voice; for it rose from a place where men and women, who like himself believed in the Eternal One and who adored the Almighty Lord, were daily slaughtered like cattle. And this foreman who was forced to help the SS murderers take his fellow Jews to their doom, this strong man who, at first glance, seemed ready for anything, never once in his innermost soul renounced the faith of his fathers. At this moment he must have been alone among Jews all over the world to praise **God's** name in a place where that name was desecrated in the vilest possible manner. To me Fischl seemed a creature from another world, a world solely ruled and embodied by a God whom I sought in vain to comprehend in Auschwitz.

To begin with our fears that presently we might have to return to the crematorium in order to dispose of the corpses of Jews who had been gassed the day before proved unfounded. We stayed in our cell for three days. On the fourth day we were awakened at the crack of dawn by Stark's terrifying voice yelling from the yard: 'Fischl team, get ready!' Our working party had been given a title.

It was dawn, a few hours before roll-call, when we entered the crematorium yard. The prisoners in the camp were still asleep. But the SS men with their machine-guns in their watch-towers were particularly vigilant at that hour, for it was at break of day that prisoners would decide upon the only way of escape: across the prohibited area into the high-tension barbed-wire fence.

Oberscharführer Quackernack turned up with several young *SS-Unterführers*. Today, we noticed, they did not carry any truncheons. Once more we had to stand by the wall beneath the window of the cremation room. For a few minutes there was tense silence. Then we heard the noise of trucks approaching. They stopped outside the crematorium yard, the engines were switched off and all was silent once more until the two halves of the wooden gate were opened. A procession of a few hundred middle-aged men and women entered the yard. Once again there was also a sprinkling of old people and children. Peaceably they came in, showing none of the signs of utter exhaustion we had observed in the people of a few days earlier. Their SS escorts, too, behaved differently: there was no shouting, no goading, guns were carefully tucked away in their pockets, and not a word of abuse passed their lips. The guards at the gate were becoming impatient. They thought the prisoners could smell a rat; the column was walking far too slowly, and before they could close the gate they had to wait until the very last person, a little one-legged man limping on crutches, had reached the yard.

We, too, thought the surprisingly gentle demeanour of the SS men very odd indeed. They looked amiable, they behaved affably, directing people like traffic policemen to get them distributed right across the yard. Some of the arrivals looked around curiously but also somehow alarmed before putting down their small suitcases, rucksacks and parcels. They spoke Polish and Yiddish. I was able to catch a few words and learned that these people had been working in a factory. From there they were deported quite suddenly, supposedly for important work using their special skills. Although the behaviour of the SS men gave them no cause for alarm, the locked yard made them suspicious and afraid. The main subject of their conversation was work, for they were all skilled workers, and death, for they were fully aware of their situation and were anxiously looking for some glimmer of hope. Would they be given an opportunity of doing something useful? For life in the ghetto – and their yellow Stars of David indicated that it was thence they had come – had taught them that only the useful had a chance of survival.

And how were we to act in this situation? Was there anything at all we could do? For we knew only too well what was going to happen to these people within the next hour. We stood rooted against the wall, paralysed by a feeling of impotence and the certainty of their and our inexorable fate. Alas, there was no power on earth which could have saved these poor innocent wretches. They had been condemned to death by a megalomaniac dictator who had set himself up to be judge and jury. Hitler and his henchmen had never made a secret of their attitude to the Jews nor of their avowed intention to exterminate them like vermin. The whole world knew it, and knowing it remained silent; was not their silence equivalent to consent? It was considerations like these which led my companions and me to the conviction that the world consented to what was happening here before our eyes.

Would anything have been changed in the course of events if any of us had stepped out and, facing the crowd, had shouted: 'Do not be deceived, men and women, you are taking your last walk, a terrible death in the gas chamber awaits you!' The majority would not have believed us because it was too terrible to be believed. On the other hand a warning like this would have led to a panic, ending in a bloody massacre and our certain death. Did we have the right to take such a risk and, in taking it, to gamble away our chance to go on living for the time being? What, at that moment, was more important: a few hundred men and women, still alive but facing imminent death from which there was no saving them, or a handful of eyewitnesses, one or two of whom might, at the price of suffering and denial of self, survive to bear witness against the murderers some day?

All at once the crowd fell silent. The gaze of several hundred pairs of eyes turned upwards to the flat roof of the crematorium. Up there, immediately above the entrance to the crematorium, stood Aumeier, flanked by Grabner, and by Hössler who later was put in charge of the women's camp. Aumeier spoke first. His voice thick with booze, he talked persuasively to these frightened, alarmed and doubt-racked people. 'You have come here,' he began, 'to work in the same way as our soldiers who are fighting at the front. Anybody who is able and willing to work will be all right.' After Aumeier it was Grabner's turn. He asked the people to get undressed because, in their own interest, they had to be disinfected. 'First and foremost we shall have to see that you are healthy,' he said. 'Therefore everyone will have to take a shower. Now, when you've had your showers, there'll be a bowl of soup waiting for you all.' Life flooded back into the upturned faces of the men and women listening eagerly to every word. The desired effect had been achieved: initial suspicion gave way to hope, perhaps even to the belief that everything might still end happily. Hössler sensing the change of mood quickly began to speak. In order to invest this large-scale deception with the semblance of complete honesty, he put on a perfect act to delude these unsuspecting people. 'You over there in the corner,' he cried, pointing at a little man, 'what's your trade?' 'I'm a tailor,' came the prompt reply. 'Ladies' or gents'?' inquired Hössler. 'Both,' the little man replied confidently. 'Excellent!' Hössler was delighted. 'That's precisely the sort of people we need in our workrooms. When you've had your shower, report to me at once. And you over there, what can you do?' He turned to a good-looking middle-aged woman who was standing right in front. 'I am a trained nurse, sir,' she replied. 'Good for you, we urgently need nurses in our hospital, and if there are any more trained nurses among you, please report to me immediately after your shower.'

Now it was Grabner's turn again. 'We need craftsmen of all kinds, fitters, electricians, motor mechanics, welders, bricklayers and cement mixers; you must all report. But we'll also need unskilled helpers. Everybody is going to get well-paid work here.' And he finished with the words: 'Now get undressed quickly, otherwise your soup will get cold.'

All the people's fears and anxieties had vanished as if by magic. Quiet as lambs they undressed without having to be shouted at or beaten. Each tried his or her best to hurry up with their undressing so that they might be among the first to get under the shower. After a very short time the yard was empty but for shoes, clothing, underwear, suit-cases and boxes which were strewn all over the ground. Cozened and deceived, hundreds of men, women and children had walked, innocently and without a struggle, into the large windowless chamber of the crematorium. When the last one had crossed the threshold, two SS men slammed shut the heavy iron-studded door which was fitted with a rubber seal, and bolted it.

Meanwhile, the *Unterführers* on duty had gone onto the crematorium roof, from where the three SS leaders had addressed the crowd. They removed the covers from the six camouflaged openings. Then, protected by gas-masks, they poured the green-blue crystals of the deadly gas into the gas chamber.

At Grabner's command the engines of the trucks still standing near by were turned on. Their noise was to prevent anyone in the camp from hearing the shouting and the banging on the doors of the dying in the gas chamber. We, however, were spared nothing, but had to witness everything in close proximity. It was as though Judgment Day had come. We could clearly hear heart-rending weeping, cries for help, fervent prayers, violent banging and knocking and, drowning everything, the noise of truck engines running at top speed. Aumeier, Grabner and Hössler were checking by their watches the time it took for the noise inside the gas chamber to cease, cracking macabre jokes while they were waiting, like 'The water in the showers must be very hot to make them scream so loudly.' Their triumphant faces showed clearly that they were delighted with the easy victory they had today scored over the declared arch-enemy of the Third Reich. When the groans and death-rattles had stopped the engines were switched off. One more mission in the campaign called *Sonderbehandlung** (Special Treatment) had been successfully completed.

Shortly afterwards camp life awoke to a new day. Ration carriers were lugging vats of tea into the barracks, senior prisoners were busy getting ready for counting roll-call, *Kapos* were assigning prisoners to working parties, and from the camp we could hear the rousing music of the camp orchestra sending the prisoners off to work.

Aumeier and his underlings had climbed down from the roof. With some considerable pride he turned to Stark and Quackernack who were walking by his side and remarked like a master addressing his apprentices: 'Well, you two, have you got it now? That's the way to do it!'

Afterwards this technique was used as a reliable method for the mass extermination of human beings without bloodshed, and it began to assume monstrous proportions. From the end of May 1942 one transport after another vanished in this way into the crematorium of Auschwitz.

At the same time, the siting of the crematorium in the immediate vicinity of the camp was fraught with danger: there was the distinct possibility that The Secret Matter of the Reich could not remain hushed up forever, notwithstanding its top-secret classification. It was for this reason that the columns of deported Jews were conducted to the 'showers' either at daybreak when the camp inmates were still asleep, or late at night after roll-call. On these occasions a camp curfew was declared. To break it meant to risk being shot. For that same reason those of us prisoners who had been forced to participate in preparations for the extermination of Jews as well as in covering up all traces of the crimes were divided into two groups. This was to prevent us from pooling our information and obtaining detailed knowledge of the extermination methods. Prisoners of the second working party, the crematorium stokers, turned up only after we had swept and thoroughly cleaned the yard. By the time they arrived the gas chamber had already been aired and the gassed were lying there as if they had just fallen naked from the sky.

Quite soon the SS men realized that they could hide nothing

from us. Our two groups were amalgamated and became the crematorium working party, with Mietek, a political prisoner from Poland, as *Kapo*. If no transport had arrived by dawn we would leave our cell in Block 11 and join the stokers in the yard. Their *Kapo* with his two assistants slept in a 'free' block, while the three Jewish stokers lived in Block 11. Lined up like a work column we stood ready waiting for the signal to march off to work. This gave us a chance to speak to other prisoners and to establish contacts with the world of the 'free' camp, a great boost for our morale, isolated as we were.

Before we set out to work the *Kapo*s of the different work teams ran round their groups straightening their lines and painstakingly counting the prisoners to make sure the number of their 'sheep' tallied with that of the SS man in charge. The camp orchestra struck up and to the sound of military music the working teams left for their place of work led by their *Kapo* who reported work assignment and number of prisoners in his column to the *Arbeitsdienst** leader. Team after team thus marched through the main gate out of the camp in rank and file, an army of thousands of slaves in striped prison uniforms. Their forced labour had been organized in such a way that, directly or indirectly, it contributed towards their own destruction.

The prisoners of the motor transport team, for instance, repaired and serviced the trucks belonging to the SS which carried not only the materials for building work in the camp, but also the living and the dead to the crematorium. The building team made the concrete posts for the endless fences and the fitters put up the barbed wire. The electricians wired it up for high tension, thus drawing ever more tightly the net in which they and their fellow sufferers were entrapped. The wooden gate to the crematorium and the great door which hermetically sealed the gas chamber had been made by prisoner carpenters. Prisoner plumbers had laid a water-pipe inside the crematorium and repaired it when necessary to prevent the death factory from going out of operation. Prisoner bricklayers replaced the round chimney which had been destroyed during the crematorium blaze by a tall new square chimney. Prisoner carters with their horses and carts fetched coke and wood for the cremation of the murder victims and carried away their clothes and belongings. But it was not only heavy physical work with which prisoners were forced to contribute to their own destruction. In the chaos which was Auschwitz, where human beings died like flies, prisoners were manipulated and drawn into the process of violent death in such ways that from the first the Nazis enforced their participation in wholesale mass murder.

Joining forces with the stokers freed us from our hopeless isolation. However, we soon realized that we were threatened by an unforeseen danger. It came, not from the SS, but from one of our own ranks, from our *Kapo*, Mietek. He had been only twenty years old when he was deported to Auschwitz in the autumn of 1940. On his tunic he wore the red triangle of the political prisoner: in Auschwitz this gave him a certain prestige. Under the influence of the camp atmosphere young Mietek had turned into a sadistic brute. But it was exclusively his Jewish fellow prisoners who were the butt of his brutal attacks. In the course of his daily contact with the SS he had become convinced that whatever happened inside as well as outside the camp was the fault of the Jews. Above all – as the Nazi propaganda machine never ceased asserting – it was the Jews who had instigated the war, and they must therefore be held responsible for all the suffering it was bringing down upon mankind. His exaggerated nationalism and his hatred of the Jews had turned this crematorium team *Kapo* into a murderer much feared by his fellow prisoners. He served the SS executioners with the devoted passion of a chauvinist fanatic. A favourite of both Grabner and Quackernack, he grew steadily more brutal and arrogant. Already during the first few days after the Fischl team had joined forces with the stoker team there was a serious quarrel between our foreman and the Polish *Kapo*. Both insisted on being Number One. Mietek had the support of the political department of the Gestapo and of the two Poles working with him in the crematorium. Fischl's support was *Lagerführer* Aumeier. In addition to the five of us in Fischl's team there were also the three Jewish stokers in Mietek's team who took Fischl's part. They told us how harshly and cruelly Mietek treated them and how many innocent prisoners had been put to death by the blond Pole.

Soon after we joined forces with his team he tried to finish off one of us, but Fischl stood up to him and prevented it. Thus in the summer of 1942 there were effectively two *Kapos* in the Auschwitz crematorium, Mietek, the official *Kapo*, and Fischl who had gained his authority by being strong and unafraid. While inside the gas chamber innocent victims were coughing up their souls, the two

*Kapo*s wrangled and fought about their prestige and over who was to be in charge.

Towards the end of the summer Fischl died of typhus. His life even before his detention in Auschwitz had been an uninterrupted chain of shocks and tragic experiences. But the 23-year-old did not succumb. Hardened by his experiences he learned to manage in the most terrible situations. Soon after the Nazi invasion of Poland his father was shot without reason by Nazi soldiers outside his butcher's shop. His mother died of grief soon afterwards. Young Fischl was arrested and put into prison for alleged black-marketeering. A few months later, without trial or sentence, he was deported to Auschwitz. He was taken to the crematorium only a few hours before me. *Lagerführer* Aumeier had selected him when looking for 'strong men for pleasant work'. Without hesitating for a moment Fischl had volunteered, but when he walked through the crematorium gate and was faced with piles of dead bodies in the cremation room he was no less shocked than we were to be later. But he had been taught earlier on that anyone revolting against the SS was writing his own death warrant. In prison he not only came to know the mentality of SS men but he also learned how to conform and win their favour. From the start he never showed the least indecision, fear, or lack of self-confidence. He reacted instantly and promptly to every command by an SS man, doing as he was bid as though what happened in the crematorium was normal routine work. Within a few hours he had acquired astonishing skill in the process of cremating corpses while, by pretending to be a brute who was eager and ready for anything, he had managed to gain the liking, one might almost say the favour, of the all-powerful Aumeier. He was playing a dangerous game, but he played it in a masterly fashion. He was just as masterful in his role as the harsh and cruel Mietek and yet he never once jeopardized our health or well-being, let alone our lives. Fischl was no angel, but neither was he a murderer, and after his death not one of us succeeded in gaining anything like the authority he had held or in creating a counterbalance to the ruthlessness of Mietek.

Once Fischl was dead Mietek threw away any scruples he might still have had. He would fly into an uncontrollable rage if, in his view, we had failed to clean one of the bicycles belonging to the SS to the degree of perfection he expected. And he would go berserk if he found the most minute trace of blood on the thoroughly scrubbed cobblestones with which the crematorium yard was paved. When there were no corpses to cremate, his underlings were not allowed to remain idle. He would think up something with which to keep us on the trot. We were made to sweep, clean and polish and he checked everything with an eagle eye. Every nook and cranny in the cremation room was closely inspected. He particularly enjoyed running his fingertips over the cast-iron valves and fittings of the ovens. Any speck of dust would immediately throw him into a paroxysm of fury. After a string of obscene invective and anti-Semitic threats he would ask the 'culprit' to own up. When he had established who the 'guilty' person was he would command: 'Maurice, bring the stool!' The prisoner found guilty by Mietek was made to lie across the wooden stool which Maurice had fetched. And then he would receive a beating, usually twenty-five strokes on the bare behind. The first few strokes were always the worst and most of the 'criminals' soiled themselves. More experienced prisoners clenched their teeth in an effort to bear the first furious violent blows without visible emotion because, quite soon afterward, the *Kapo*'s rage would abate. If a man could stand the first few blows without making a sound, Mietek would say in Polish: 'You son of a bitch, you'll only get fifteen because you didn't whine.' New prisoners who screamed, writhed with pain and leapt off the stool at the first few blows, or who dropped to their knees and, with raised hands, implored Mietek for mercy, only succeeded in increasing his fury. He rained blows on them indiscriminately, beating them on their hands or about the head; the more a prisoner writhed with pain the more brutal the *Kapo*'s thrashing, and not infrequently he beat them to death. Within a very few days he had in this way reduced the number of his first team of Jewish helpers from eight to six. The murdered men were replaced by two new prisoners from the next transport of Jews.

Mietek differed from the rest of the prisoners not only on account of his brutality but also because he was a dandy. He invariably wore a clean made-to-measure uniform, and a clean shirt daily which contributed not a little towards his dandified appearance. Watching him chat almost amicably with his Polish companions or listening to him talking in a group of camp leaders it was difficult to believe that this man could change, at the drop of a hat, into a homicidal maniac. Mietek enjoyed a special relationship with *Unterscharführer* Lorenz, one of Gestapo chief

Grabner's subordinates. With his black gypsy moustache and somewhat advanced in years, Lorenz appeared to be an affable and good-natured man. He spoke Polish fluently and talked to Mietek exclusively in his mother tongue. He in turn addressed the SS man informally, indeed almost affectionately, as *dziaduno*, or grandpa. Lorenz turned up in the crematorium almost daily, sometimes even several times a day, to find out whether Mietek had managed to *organize* anything for him and his cronies of the political department. Obviously Mietek excelled here as well, for this was the only feasible explanation for the unusually intimate relationship between a prisoner and an *SS-Unterführer*.

After each demonstration of his strength and authority Mietek noted down the number of the prisoner killed and went to the Gestapo quarters near by in order to report a reduction in his numbers and to put in for a replacement. At first an SS man would appear to check the identity of the prisoner killed. Later on no one came any more, for in the meantime the crematorium *Kapo* had won the full confidence of his superiors in the SS. With his two Polish mates, Mietek's quarters were in Block 15, right among the camp notables, while we continued to dwell in isolation in Block 11.

It was in the late autumn of 1942 that we noticed the absence of *Unterscharführer* Stark. At first we tried to guess whether he might be ill and likely to return or whether he had been transferred. When he had still not returned a week later it was rumoured that he had been transferred to the front. Some people claimed to know that he had been given study leave. Anyway, from that time on we never set eyes on him again and everybody was glad to see the back of him.

The killing of innocent victims in the gas chamber was not the only means of mass murder in the crematorium of Auschwitz. In the gas chamber of the crematorium – we used to call it the mortuary – they practised another kind of execution, one that we had often witnessed at the black wall of Block 11. If a transport of less than 200 people arrived for liquidation then, as a rule, they were killed not by gassing but by a bullet through the base of the skull. In that event Mietek and his two helpers led one doomed person after another to the panelled wall of the mortuary where they held them with a grip of steel. As on the production line of a slaughter-house, members of the SS, such as Palitzsch, Stark, Dylewski and Quackernack, put them to death with a shot through the base of the skull from their silenced small-bore rifles. If it was Jews who were done away with in this manner, Mietek did not care. Calm and composed he led them to their execution. But tears were in his eyes if it was a batch of 'Aryan' Poles he had to escort on their last journey. After such an execution he would behave like a madman. Trembling with rage and agitation he'd yell at us: 'You fucking Yid bastards, it's all your fault that my countrymen are being killed!' And then he'd fling himself on the nearest Jewish prisoner and beat him to death. Often his two Polish companions tried to calm him down and stop him from going berserk. But it was no good, and in the end they shut up because they feared that in his blind rage he might attack them.

It may be hard to comprehend how quickly the characters of many prisoners tended to change in the atmosphere in which we lived. But neither intelligence nor education was a bulwark against the distortion of a man's personality or of his intrinsic character, and the Cracow student, Mieczislaw, was a typical example for the truth of this assertion.

I did not learn until much later the circumstances to which Mietek owed his 'career' as a *Kapo*. Before he came to the crematorium it had been one of his duties to clean the bicycles of the political department. He must have impressed Gestapo chief Grabner with his zeal and eagerness, his punctiliousness and reliability, to such an extent that he appointed him crematorium *Kapo*.

The crematorium ovens were also used for the dead of other camp areas. Each evening the corpses of those who had died in the camp hospital arrived on a trolley. These were mainly *Mussulmans*. That was the name given to prisoners who had spiritually and, above all, physically, completely deteriorated. They had become nothing but skin and bones. Often their bones had rubbed through their thin parchment-like skin, resulting in inflamed and festering wounds. They had either died of exhaustion or they had been killed by a phenol injection. Sometimes there were also victims of pseudo-medical experiments.

The bearers who had to push the trolley from the hospital building to the crematorium yard were dressed in white. Usually there were six or seven of them. To unload, two climbed up on the trolley and threw the dead bodies on the ground. One grabbed them by the wrists, the other by the heels. They swung them to and fro a few times until they had gathered enough momentum.

Then they let go so that the corpse hit the ground with a smack. There was an eery sound when on impact air escaped from mouth or anus. While the remaining carriers were busy dragging corpses into the crematorium, the pavement was constantly kept wet so that their burdens might slide more easily along the ground. As soon as all the corpses had been taken to the crematorium the carriers cleaned the yard before returning the trolley to the hospital building. Some of the corpses were horrible to look at. Often they had been dismembered or dissected. Many were the bodies of young men and women who bore strange burns and festering wounds on their testicles or the lower parts of their bodies, or abcesses on their bellies and thighs. Yet others had taken on a pinky-bluish hue, or they had purple faces and clenched jaws. In addition there were all those who had been killed by shooting in the yard of Block 11; they too were taken to the crematorium.

Almost every night a truck trailer was parked in the crematorium yard. It was piled high with the corpses of prisoners who had died or been killed in the concentration camp of Birkenau. In the morning we had to unload it. All we had to do was to wind up the front end of the loading space until the corpses slid down the back and dropped on the pavement. But even we, the hardened prisoners of the *Sonderkommando*, invariably shuddered at the sight of corpses which from time to time were brought to the crematorium from Katowice. They came in wooden boxes and were delivered by a car of the Katowice Gestapo. When the boxes were opened we usually found two pale, bloodless bodies at whose feet lay their decapitated heads. One of these particularly gruesome corpses was the dead body of the German mayor of Auschwitz. At first his corpse was not released for cremation. Permission was given only after it had been inspected by several SS men of the political department. We learned from Quackernack that the mayor had been found guilty of irregularities.

From time to time SS doctors visited the crematorium, above all *Hauptsturmführer* Kitt and *Obersturmführer** Weber. During their visits it was just like working in a slaughterhouse. Like cattle dealers they felt the thighs and calves of men and women who were still alive and selected what they called the best pieces before the victims were executed. After their execution the chosen bodies were laid on a table. The doctors proceeded to cut pieces of still warm flesh from thighs and calves and threw them into waiting receptacles. The muscles of those who had been shot were still working and contracting, making the bucket jump about. At first we thought the Nazis planned to use human flesh for plastic operations on wounded soldiers. Only later we learned that these buckets of living flesh were taken to the Institute of Hygiene at Rajsko where it was used in the laboratories for the growing of bacterial cultures. Once I heard *Oberscharführer* Quackernack remark: 'Horseflesh would do, but in war-time it is too valuable for that sort of thing.'

The continuous operation of the crematorium and, most of all, the overloading of the ovens – an aspect not taken into account during their construction – led to the crumbling of the fire-bricks of the inner lining, so that there was a danger of the chimney collapsing. Therefore, in the summer of 1942 a new square chimney with a double lining of fire-bricks was added. However, operations in the crematorium continued without interruption while this work was carried out.

A team of about thirty was building the new chimney, the majority of them Jewish prisoners. One, who came from Slovakia like myself, told me that my father was in a transport which had recently arrived from the concentration camp of Lublin. At once I began a hectic search for him. When I had found out in which block he was housed I managed, with the help of dollars and diamonds I had *organized*, to bribe the *Kapo* of the bricklayers' team. He agreed to include my father in the team which was working on the chimney. One morning as I was busy removing cinders on a wheelbarrow I met my father in the *Kapo*'s little wooden hut. He neither knew nor suspected what kind of work his son was engaged in. In a state of happy excitement at seeing me again, he embraced me, stroking my cheeks and repeating over and over, his voice trembling with emotion: 'My dear boy, I was looking for you all over the place and felt sure I would find you among the musicians of the camp orchestra. I knew that's where you'd be.' Then he turned to a prisoner who was standing next to him and added with satisfaction tinged with a certain pride: 'What a good thing that my Filip is such a splendid fiddle player. At least that'll save him from the worst.'

I could not bear to stay any longer. What could I have said to my father, this good and honest Jew who still put his trust in the truthfulness of his fellow men? What could I have said to him who, sickened by the plots of the fascist Hlinka Guards of Slovakia, had volunteered for one of the transports to the East as early as February 1942? And why had he done so? In order, as he said with the true ring of conviction, to help create a new life for his family there. And now, as we were meeting, he tried to stifle his deep disappointment. Striving to ignore evil and wickedness he forced himself to go on believing in his ideas which, alas, were no more than pious wishes. I felt like shouting: 'You are mistaken, father! Your son Filip, the promising grammar-school boy, the budding violinist, is not a musician but one who cremates corpses. Do you hear me, father! Your son Filip is a stoker in the crematorium!' But my throat was so tight, I could not utter a word. My eyes brimming with tears I rushed from the dark hut. Grabbing the empty wheelbarrow I ran to the crematorium gate. And high time too, for Mietek Morawa was inquiring where I was.

I met my father a few more times. Despite all the help and assistance I managed to give him I perceived that he was hardly able to keep on his feet. I saw that he was feverish. From his unnaturally bright eyes and cracked lips it was easy to diagnose that he had typhus. A few days later when the trolley arrived from the hospital, my father's body was among the dead. My fellow prisoners bore his corpse to the crematorium and placed it on the trolley in the cremation room. In front of the blazing ovens a team-mate recited the Kaddish. Steadfast in his belief, calm, imperturbable and true to the ancient tradition of his forefathers, he praised his Lord: 'May the great name of the Lord be exalted and hallowed throughout the world which he hath created according to his will. May he establish his kingdom in your days, in your days and in the days of all the house of Israel speedily! And say ye, Amen.'

I had come to believe that there were no human feelings left inside me. But while my team-mate recited the Kaddish my soul mourned in pain and grief. As the flames busily devoured the mortal remains of my father, the words of the traditional prayer gave me solace in this hour of sorrow.

Chapter 3
The new death factories

The building works department of the SS had expected that, once the new square chimney was built, operations would run smoothly and without a hitch. However, it turned out quite soon that this new chimney could not cope with the work-load: while it was in use, lining bricks kept coming loose, blocking the flue. It was no longer possible to 'despatch' the transports of Jews which continued to arrive as before without constantly recurring technical trouble. Therefore, in the autumn of 1942 operations had to be restricted. From the start this small 'death workshop', into whose gas chamber more than 700 people could be crammed, served to relieve the two extermination centres at Birkenau. Known as Bunker 1 and 2 these were two whitewashed farmhouses with thatched roofs, all that remained of the village of Brzezinka. Converted into gas chambers they were sited to the west of the future crematoria 4 and 5.

The people gassed here were simply buried in mass graves which had been dug near by. When, in the summer of 1942, the hot sun began to burn, the corpses started to swell and the earth's crust to burst open. A black, evil-smelling mass oozed out and polluted the ground-water in the vicinity. One day we were ordered to take several barrels of chlorinated lime there. Large quantities of this chemical were spread over the decomposing bodies, but to no avail. For, when in October 1942 we returned to the pits with several containers of oil, I managed to speak to a few prisoners of the *Sonderkommando* there. The majority were Slovak Jews, a few came from France. They were busy digging up and burning the decomposing corpses. This ghoulish work took place in an area enveloped in black smoke and acrid fumes. At the edge of the mass grave lay a heap of blue-black bodies covered with maggots. They were flung on trucks by a group of prisoners. A second group moved these to a pit where the bodies were burnt.

Among the prisoners working here I recognized two friends with whom I had been at grammar school. From them I learned that they had been working at the bunkers since the spring of 1942. But bodies had been buried in mass graves even earlier, for there was a first *Sonderko.nmando* of eighty who, as they were privy to the mass extermination, had all been liquidated by *Hauptscharführer** Moll. While we were talking a couple of SS men appeared and separated us. Obviously they did not know that I was among those who knew about their secret.

In mid-December 1942 all who belonged to this *Sonderkommando* were gassed and cremated. On removing their bodies from the gas chamber we found on some of them scraps of paper with notes scribbled on them to the effect that their plan to escape had been betrayed by certain barrack orderlies.

Despite constant trouble with the chimney, the Auschwitz crematorium remained in use. During the first few months of 1943 it served simultaneously as a training centre for a new team of stokers. They were to be employed in the crematoria of Birkenau which were then being built. About twenty Jewish and three Polish prisoners were instructed in the duties of a crematorium worker by *Kapo* Mietek. Most of them had come towards the end of 1942 from the ghetto of the Polish town of Ciechanow. Their subsequent fate was decided when their transport arrived on the ramp at Auschwitz. For this happened to be the day when the SS men on duty were selecting more slaves for the new *Sonderkommando*, which they did by placing the youngest, healthiest and strongest males on one side.

In the end there were three groups on the ramp. The first contained mainly women with small children, as well as middle-aged and old people; in the second group were young men and girls as well as women without children; while about 200 strong men had been selected for the third. None of them could imagine what this sorting into three groups might mean. Had the women and children been put together so that the mothers could look after their little ones; were the younger ones intended for normal work and the strong and healthy men for heavy physical labour? When they saw women, children and older folk climbing into trucks and being driven away their hopes of staying with their families were dashed. Later they were taken to the camp where they encountered older prisoners and had their first sobering experience: one of them, a student who was being trained as a stoker in the Auschwitz crematorium, told me how, when he inquired after his relatives, he had been informed quite cynically and with complete indifference that they had long since snuffed it. Others had similar experiences and, as a result, were completely stunned and shocked during their first few days. However, once they had recovered, they would begin to speculate about their own chances of survival. They knew full well where they were and what they might expect. And yet, in his heart of hearts every man hoped that he would be the one lucky enough to get out of here alive.

To fill up empty places in the *Sonderkommando* the SS employed all manner of deceptions. A friend of mine was among the many prisoners taken in by their tricks. One day he was told that strong and healthy men were wanted for well-paid work in the Bata shoe factory 200 kilometres away. Eagerly and suspecting nothing he volunteered for this work. When a little later he was taken to the crematorium he realized that he had been tricked: but by then it was too late.

Rumours that the new crematoria at Birkenau would soon be completed increased. By mid-July 1943 they were ready. The old crematorium at Auschwitz was shut down. Eight SS men of Ukrainian origin were among the last to be cremated there. Because of their nationality they had feared that one day they might be gassed or shot; they managed to escape but were pursued into the mountains where they were cornered, and during the ensuing gunfight all eight of them were killed. When one of our team was searching their pockets for cigarettes he found three 'pineapples'. He hid them in an empty urn. But then we were suddenly transferred, and there was no time for anyone to collect the hand-grenades. We had to leave them behind until a week later when we managed to smuggle them into Birkenau. They were the first weapons we managed to lay our hands on.

The old death factory of Auschwitz stood empty and silent as the grave. Tens of thousands of Jews from Upper Silesia, Slovakia, France, Holland, Yugoslavia and the ghettos of Theresienstadt, Ciechanow and Grodno had been put to death and cremated there, and their ashes scattered in the river Vistula. Occasionally an urn, supposedly containing the ashes of a dead prisoner was sent to his relatives – as long as he was not a Jew – against payment of a fee. Needless to say they were never the remains of any particular person: the urn was simply filled with a handful of ashes of which there was always a plentiful supply.

We were no longer needed here. That we had a chance to go on living, however, was due solely to the fact that the four new crematoria at Birkenau were now in operation.

We bid farewell to the bunker trusty of Block 11 who was known as Bunker-Jacob. Jacob had come to Auschwitz at the beginning of 1943. He was a giant of a man, athletic and brawny. Rumour had it that he used to be a sparring partner of Max Schmeling, the famous German heavyweight boxer. At Auschwitz he used to give displays of his muscle power on Sunday afternoons when, outside the prison kitchen, in front of thousands of prisoners and numerous SS men, he would bend iron rods with his bare hands. It was his strength which had gained him the respect of the SS. It had also gained him the job as prison trusty in Bunker 11 (the cells in the basement of Block 11), where they could do with a strong man like Jacob, particularly on those occasions when prisoners had to be led out from the bunker to be shot in front of the black wall. And yet, Jacob was one of those men of athletic build who are often characterized by their outstanding helpfulness and good nature. We were not the only ones who owed him a great improvement in our living conditions since his arrival in Block 11. Every Sunday following afternoon roll-call he let us out of the block, not without first urging us to tell everyone in the camp exactly what was going on here.

When I came to Birkenau I could not at first believe the change which had taken place in the marshy landscape which, only fifteen months earlier, had been desolate and empty. In addition to the small B1 sector where I had spent a few days in the early April of 1942, a second one had sprung up. With its seven almost completed camps and about 200 barracks it was another slave town.

After our transfer we were assigned to this new B2d camp, with our living quarters in Block 13. At first glance this was in no way different from all the other barracks. Its exterior reminded one of a stable rather than a human habitation. Our barrack was about 40 metres long and 10 metres wide. But unlike the other yards ours was surrounded by a wall. The door in this wall was almost always locked. The only exit was through a door in the front. It was guarded by a prisoner who was young and strong and armed with a wooden stick. It was his business to see that nobody from the outside had any contact with the prisoners who lived here and who were in on the secret.

The block was ruled by Serge, a Paris textile merchant of Polish origin. He had arrived at the camp towards the end of March 1942. The sleeve of his prison uniform was adorned by a red armband on which *Senior – Block 13* could be read. About thirty and of medium height, he had an unusually red face and sported wide-rimmed spectacles which would have been more suited to a Left-Bank intellectual. Although I was only an ordinary prisoner, while he was one who wielded a good deal of influence, he was very kind to me simply because the numbers with which we were both tattooed were very similar. Among prisoners in this concentration camp those with 'old' numbers automatically commanded great respect. There were about 400 prisoners in our block, mainly Polish Jews from the ghetto of Ciechanow and the camp at Kielbasin, in addition to a group of French Jews of Polish origin from the camp at Drancy, with a few Jews from Holland, Greece and Slovakia.

After almost fourteen months of isolation in Block 11, living together with my fellow prisoners gave me a feeling of solidarity because we shared the same fate. I no longer felt quite as forlorn and despondent as before. Although this new block was isolated from the rest of the camp, compared to it our bunker cell in Block 11 at Auschwitz had been a black hole. Here I could at least get a breath of fresh air in the yard, go to the wash-room if I wanted a wash, and talk to my fellow prisoners, the majority of whom were decent and straightforward, about anything that worried and depressed me. I reckoned that we might have a chance of some kind of tolerable life together here, the more so since *Kapo* Mietek and his two Polish cronies were now quartered in Block 2 where all the nobs lived. The occasional contact with prisoners outside the block – though, of course, strictly forbidden – but also the more humane attitude of our four *Kapos*, led me once more to think about my future, and to ponder on the amazing resilience of human nature: for the monstrous mass destruction had by no means ceased; our own deaths seemed certain and indeed imminent; and yet, even the slightest improvement in our living conditions was enough for all this to be pushed into the background.

There were other things which had changed for the better.

Jewish doctors were now permitted to work in the camp hospital alongside their Polish colleagues. Elsewhere Jewish block seniors, clerks and orderlies were given more important jobs. When the work teams marched out there were, now and then, *Kapos* and foremen wearing the Star of David, something which would have been impossible in 1942.

The reason for this development lay obviously in the military and economic situation of the Third Reich which was growing more and more unfavourable. There were noticeable improvements for us particularly after the defeat of the German armies at Stalingrad. At Auschwitz and its adjoining camps large numbers of industrial concerns, each one most vital to the war effort, were springing up all the time, among them the Buna Works, the Vistula Union Metal Works, and the German Munition Works. Since each of these factories was expected to turn out its goods with the utmost efficiency, those in charge of the camp were faced with the necessity of keeping alive a sufficiently large reservoir of prisoners to provide a cheap work-force. In the face of the precarious military and economic situation, the extermination of prisoners through senseless forced labour could no longer be condoned. That meant the end of entertainments such as making prisoners transfer heaps of sand from one place to another and back again by transporting their load in the front flap of their shirts and, needless to say, at the double. This game was repeated *ad lib* and regularly resulted in the collapse and death of a number of prisoners. The place of such sadistic excesses was taken by what became known as *extermination through labour*.

Even if the cynical attitude of the SS towards us prisoners remained unchanged, the new situation did, to a certain extent, operate in our favour. With the help of luck, skill and bribery those who were healthy and able to work had at least a sporting chance to keep going for a time. Admittedly, after some months the combination of heavy slave labour and insufficient food of about 1,200 calories daily resulted in the majority of prisoners wasting away. And once a prisoner had spent all his energies, so that he could no longer be used as a slave labourer, to the gas chamber he would go.

Under these new, albeit harsh, living conditions the death rate among Jewish prisoners, compared to 1942, had decreased significantly so that now they represented a not insignificant proportion of camp inmates. Moreover, non-Jewish prisoners were increasingly transferred to Buchenwald or other camps. This was bound to bring about changes particularly in the prisoner hierarchy, and Jewish prisoner functionaries were now no longer an unusual phenomenon.

I shared a bunk with another prisoner on the top tier, which was the best spot, for there was nobody above you. On the bunk next to mine slept Daniel Obstbaum. He was about thirty-five, and an uncommonly intelligent and serious man. He came from France where he had been a skilled worker in a reserved occupation in an aircraft factory. Arrested for distributing anti-Nazi leaflets he and his family were deported to Auschwitz where his family was sent to the gas chamber immediately on their arrival. He finally landed in the *Sonderkommando* and was foreman of a team responsible for removing corpses from the gas chamber to crematorium 4. He was always neatly turned out, as far as that was possible in a concentration camp, and would wear a dark-blue made-to-measure jacket. Only later it occurred to me that his dandified and self-assured manner might have been intended to hide his escape plans.

Daniel Obstbaum had struck up a friendship with Fero Langer, a Jewish prisoner of about twenty-eight from Slovakia. Langer was a clerk in one of the adjoining blocks. Before his deportation he had attempted to escape from Slovakia by hiding underneath a load of timber due to be exported to Switzerland. During a check at the Slovak border he was discovered by customs officials and taken to Auschwitz after his arrest. Here he met an old schoolmate called Dobrowolný, a *Volksdeutscher** who served in the camp as an SS man. The two would run into each other occasionally, and one day Dobrowolný hinted that he might not be averse to helping Langer to escape. It would be difficult, so he said, because it meant bribing a large number of SS men; for this purpose he would require diamonds, gold, dollars and other valuables.

Langer who had no access to any of these commodities now turned to Daniel Obstbaum who was prepared to *organize* them on condition that he and three of his friends would be included in the escape plans. Dobrowolný agreed; at the same time he kept pushing up his demands on account of the supposedly greater risk. Langer's contact with Dobrowolný was known to other prisoners, and he was repeatedly warned not to believe the SS man's promises; for in Auschwitz the fact that the two of them had gone to the same school and perhaps even been friends was quite meaningless. Who was there ready to swear that Dobrowolný was straight? Langer disregarded any of his companions' warnings and seemingly managed to persuade Obstbaum that Dobrowolný could be trusted. And so a day was fixed for the escape. How, and how much, the SS man was to be paid no one knew.

As arranged, one afternoon Dobrowolný led Langer, Obstbaum and three others out of the camp zone. This was not unusual, for guarded by SS men, prisoners were constantly going back and forth. However, Langer and Obstbaum made a big mistake if they believed that Dobrowolný would, as he had promised, let them go once they were outside the camp zone.

That night when we returned with the rest of the work teams, we could see from afar that near the camp orchestra some dead prisoners were on display. As we came closer we were met by a ghastly sight. Three prisoners lay on the ground while two had been sat on wooden stools. Behind them spades were thrust into the soil against which they had been propped. It was Fero Langer and Daniel Obstbaum. There eyes were wide open, staring blindly into space. Their clothing was riddled with bullet-holes and soaked in blood. Between them was a board with the inscription: 'Three cheers, we've come back again!' Dobrowolný, however, was given a week's special leave as a reward for his commendable vigilance.

In the centre of our block quite near the yard entrance slept *Kapo* Lajzer, his bum-boy,* and his 40-year-old cousin whose hand was crippled. This hand must have escaped the attention of the SS doctor on duty during the nocturnal selection procedure on the ramp. In order to keep him alive, his *Kapo* cousin made him foreman in crematorium 5, where he did not have to do any physical work. One night he told me how he had come into the *Sonderkommando*.

It was late at night when, after a whistle from the engine, the train in which he had been travelling came to a halt. They were all hustled out of their cattle trucks. Parents carried their small children in their arms and anyone with enough strength left picked up his bundle containing a few pitiful belongings. When even these were snatched from them, many thought: no matter, as long as they could stay together with their families. And then the selection began. Some were sent to the right, others to the left, and before the men had realized it, their wives, children and their old folk were separated from them and on the opposite side of the ramp. They had still not quite recovered from this first shock when their relatives were loaded on trucks and whisked away into the night. The dull sound of engines grew fainter until finally it stopped.

The following morning at the barber's came the next shock. For when they tried to find out from the prisoner barbers where their families were, they were informed in a matter-of-fact way that they would have gone up the chimney some time ago. At first they thought this a macabre joke. But afterwards they were taken to the two farmhouses. There a horde of SS men belaboured them with whips forcing them to drag corpses from a room inside the house and throw them on narrow-gauge wagons. While they were engaged in this nightmarish task the thought of what had happened to their families spun in their heads. Almost demented with fear and terror they rushed around in a daze, dragging corpses behind them without really knowing what they were doing. Like robots they kept on working. At night when they dropped on to their bunks, dead tired and exhausted, everything that had happened seemed like a long and terrible nightmare. And a few days later they ended up in that 'factory', of which they had been told before their deportation, where they were to get satisfying and well-paid work.

My first working day at Birkenau was a hot summer's day. In the early hours of the morning the work teams stood in rows on the dusty camp street, ready to march out. We were lined up near the gate, not far from the camp orchestra. Chief *Kapo*, August Brück, led the almost 200-strong crematorium team to work. This team, its *Kapos* walking in the first few ranks, was divided into four groups, one for each of the four crematoria. It was the job of a fifth group, called the demolition team, to remove any remaining traces of the cremation pits near the bunkers – no longer needed since the installation of the new crematoria – by levelling them.

Brück's tall and lean figure was striking. A *Reichsdeutscher**, he was roughly fifty years old, taciturn, and walked with a slight stoop. His face was square and wrinkled, with high cheekbones, and there was an alert look in his half-closed eyes. He had spent many years in Nazi prisons and concentration camps. In the spring of 1943 he had been transferred from Buchenwald to Birkenau where it was his job to introduce *Sonderkommando* prisoners to the installations in the new crematoria. Furthermore he was responsible for the smooth and accident-free running of the establishment.

To the sound of the camp orchestra playing a sentimental folk song we marched off to work through the main gate. A few metres behind the gate our team reformed into three independent groups. The first, turning to the left, marched towards the crematoria 4 and 5. A few metres behind walked the demolition team. The third group to which I belonged turned to the right. I noticed *Kapo* Mietek in the front rank, and my heart sank. I wondered if he would be as brutal and callous as he had been at Auschwitz.

On our way we went past the women's camp. On the left behind the barbed wire there were emaciated female figures busy loading soil into wheelbarrows. But something else attracted my attention: at the end of the camp of Birkenau behind barbed-wire fences which had been put up on either side of the dusty road, two buildings stood out clearly, and towering above them a chimney. Presently we turned to the left and through an iron gate entered a yard. The long single-storey red-brick building of crematorium 2 was only a few metres away in front of us. On one of its longer sides there was a projecting structure from which the square chimney rose up. The sight of it reminded me very forcibly of the transitoriness of life; but before long this lethal giant had become part of our daily life. Five underground channels connected it to the fifteen ovens which were arranged in groups of three.

We were divided into separate teams. At first I worked in a group of twenty; we were engaged in levelling a large mound of earth. From the surface which was to be sown with grass seed concrete shafts stuck out here and there. There could be no doubt that concealed under this mound of earth was a gas chamber.

Compared to the crematorium at Auschwitz our working conditions were noticeably less arduous. Our foreman, a young Pole, would stand there leaning on his stick without either goading or beating us. We talked to him about the latest news from the front, and at the end of each conversation he would invariably remark: 'Well, lads, it's like this: if you want to stay alive, you'll have to do something about it.' I often wondered what he was getting at, but simply could make no sense out of his enigmatic words. Only later did it dawn on me that he wanted to sound people out. But when *Oberscharführer* Voss or one of his assistants turned up, the foreman sprang into action. At once the tone of his normally quiet voice changed and he barked at us: 'Come along! Get on with your work! Make it snappy, will you!' Naturally we joined in the game and rushed around in a burst of feverish activity which created the desired impression on the watching SS bosses.

In the lunch break I ran across a mate of mine whom I had first met at the beginning of 1943, during his 'training' as a stoker in the old crematorium at Auschwitz. Through a wooden door in the left wing of the building he took me into the coke store. From there we went along a narrow semi-dark corridor, past three doors (one of which led into the *Kommandoführer*'s room) into the cremation plant. Five ovens, each with three combustion chambers, were installed here. Outwardly the fifteen arched openings did not significantly differ from those at the Auschwitz crematorium. The one important innovation consisted of two rollers, each with a diameter of 15 centimetres, fixed to the edge of each oven. This made it easier for the metal platform to be pushed inside the oven. The process of cremating corpses was similar to that in Auschwitz. The only way in which this death factory differed from the one in Auschwitz was its size. Its fifteen huge ovens, working non-stop, could cremate more than 3,000 corpses daily. Bearing in mind that scarcely more than 100 metres away there was another crematorium with the same capacity, and still another 400 metres further on the two smaller crematoria 4 and 5, with eight ovens each, one was forced to conclude that civilization had come to an end. And yet, whoever wanted to stay alive had to ignore the detestable reality and the conditions under which he was forced to live, however violently he loathed them.

Once at the crematorium I kept an eye on Mietek. Of all the *Kapos* he was the only one who wore striped prison garb. There he stood, with his arms folded, not shouting at anyone or hitting anybody, but simply attending to his job which was supervising the smooth running of the cremation plant and ensuring a continuous flow of corpses: these came up from the basement by lift. When I inquired from my mate who knew Mietek from his brief stay at Auschwitz, how Mietek treated prisoners in this place, he reassured me and said that I need have no fears. Mietek, having noticed that the other *Kapos* abhorred ill-treating prisoners, had himself stopped his brutal treatment of them. When I asked what he thought of chief *Kapo* Brück he thought he was all right. As long as he had his bottle of drink every day he was content and would leave the prisoners in peace. All this information, and most of all the fact that there would be no beatings, put my mind at rest to some extent.

Using the lift which brought the corpses up we descended into the basement. The sight of the rooms down there made me shudder. Every detail had been devised with the sole aim of cramming up to 3000 people into one room in order to kill them with poison gas. When we entered the morgue we found lying in a heap some 200 emaciated corpses, all of whom had obviously died of hunger, disease or exhaustion. They had been thrown down the concrete chute from the yard into the mortuary basement.

It was here that I met *Kapo* Kaminski. Stocky and red-faced he was about thirty-two. He had come to Birkenau with a transport from Ciechanow towards the end of 1942. Self-confident, energetic and determined, he had the courage and ability to lead others. In addition he was a man of outstanding intelligence. These qualities won him respect and recognition among the prisoners: within a short time he succeeded in holding some sort of leading position in the Birkenau *Sonderkommando*. Kaminski had a great deal of personal charm. His voice was a little hoarse, but what he said was always convincing. It was particularly in critical situations, for example when a major extermination drive was on, that he knew better than anybody else how to quieten and reassure agitated and alarmed prisoners. For a long time his manner, unafraid, determined, at times even arrogant, led the SS to believe that he was thoroughly competent to carry out his duties as a *Kapo*.

We left the mortuary and came to a huge iron-mounted wooden door; it was not locked. We entered a place which was in total darkness. As we switched on the light, the room was lit by bulbs enclosed in a protective wire cage. We were standing in a large oblong room measuring about 250 square metres. Its unusually low ceiling and walls were whitewashed. Down the length of the room concrete pillars supported the ceiling. However, not all the pillars served this purpose: for there were others, too. The Zyclon B gas crystals were inserted through openings into hollow pillars made of sheet metal. They were perforated at regular intervals and inside them a spiral ran from top to bottom in order to ensure as even a distribution of the granular crystals as possible. Mounted on the ceiling was a large number of dummy showers made of metal. These were intended to delude the suspicious on entering the gas chamber into believing that they were in a shower-room. A ventilating plant was installed in the wall; this was switched on immediately after each gassing to disperse the gas and thus to expedite the removal of corpses.

At right angles to the gas chamber was the largest room in the extermination complex, the so-called changing room. Measuring over 300 square metres, this underground room could accommodate more than 1,000 people. They entered from the yard down wide concrete steps. At the entrance to the basement was a signboard, and written on it in several languages the direction: *To the baths and disinfecting rooms*. The ceiling of the changing room was supported by concrete pillars to which many more notices were fixed, once again with the aim of making the unsuspecting people believe that the imminent process of disinfection was of vital importance for their health. Slogans like *Cleanliness brings freedom* or *One louse may kill you* were intended to hoodwink, as were numbered clothes hooks fixed at a height of 1.50 metres. Along the walls stood wooden benches, creating the impression that they were placed there to make people more comfortable while undressing. There were other multi-lingual notices inviting them to hang up their clothes as well as their shoes, tied together by their laces, and admonishing them to remember the number of their hook so that they might easily retrieve their clothes after their showers. There were further notices on the way from the changing room to the gas chamber, directing people to the baths and disinfecting room.

The whole get-up of these subterranean rooms, cunning camouflage and clumsy deception at one and the same time, was horrifying. I began to fear that what I had experienced so far was child's play to what awaited me. Every single detail was carefully aimed at allaying the victims' suspicions and calculated to take them quickly and without trouble into the gas chamber.

The number of ovens had been increased almost eightfold; the number of prisoners in the *Sonderkommando* was forty times its former strength. After initial problems had been dealt with, it was now possible in the course of twenty-four hours to cremate up to 10,000 corpses. These were, of course, not modern or technically advanced crematoria. Their operation depended entirely on slave labourers capable of doing very heavy physical work under extreme conditions.

The atmosphere in Block 13 where we were quartered was very

strange. On the one hand we had to be isolated from the rest of the camp, on the other hand, the strict observation of this isolation was supervised by other prisoners. Clearly this opened wide the doors to large-scale corruption. Every day prisoners came from the camp supplying their business partners in the *Sonderkommando* with cigarettes and alcohol in exchange for diamonds, dollars, watches, gold teeth and other valuables *organized* after gassings. There developed an illegal trade of undreamed-of dimensions where anyone who still had hopes of staying alive bartered anything that would sustain life. It was, in the main, barrack orderlies and block personnel who were involved in these activities. In return for the risks they took to keep this illegal trade going they naturally demanded their share. Frequent checks by SS leaders invariably came to nothing, although they were always carried out unexpectedly and with great thoroughness. Any hot merchandise would disappear into mysterious hiding-places. Once it had been the property of those who, in their innocent credulity, had undressed for the last time in the crematorium's changing rooms. A large part of what they left behind passed into the hands of others who were determined to survive.

Almost every prisoner in the *Sonderkommando* spent a great deal of energy on *organizing*, partly because it helped alleviate the harsh living conditions, but also because it drew our minds off the horrors around us. Besides *organizing* there was an activity known as *Auschwitz fashion* by means of which many members of the *Sonderkommando* attempted to blind themselves to their desperate situation. In order to make themselves look more like human beings they imitated their torturers by aping their way of dressing.

Then there were clandestine meetings with prisoners from the women's camp which helped many of us to forget the horror of our lives at least for a few hours. Compared to other undertakings it was, of course, uncommonly difficult for a prisoner in the *Sonderkommando* to get into the women's camp. The bribery which went on in this connection was quite unbelievable, while the men's inventiveness knew no bounds. Some managed to get inside the women's camp by joining work teams which had to do jobs there. They secured the tacit connivance of the SS men on duty at the main gate by generously greasing their palms. Still others invented the most ingenious reasons in order to reach their goal. For instance, the one and only water pump in the camp was invariably and at the most unusual hours urgently needed in the women's camp whenever it happened to be in the crematorium. In this way the heavy water pump was at regular intervals lugged back and forth between the women's camp and the crematorium. Every time there were violent arguments and power struggles concerning who was to be included in the circle of the privileged few.

The main motive for seeking these relationships with women was not so much sexual, but simply the need to have someone to care for; all family ties had been forcibly and abruptly severed, and it was this feeling of desolation, of being utterly alone in the world, which awoke in almost everyone the longing to have somebody to care for. The presents smuggled into the women's camp, whether bread, margarine, silk stockings, strange commodity in these surroundings – French perfume, had belonged to people who were no longer alive. But to those still living and suffering they gave some little solace and comfort in their daily struggle with a very harsh life.

The last row of bunks on the right at the end of our block was reserved for the sick. There was also a sort of consulting room linked to a small hospital with some twenty beds. In charge of this hospital was Dr Jacques Pach, at that time the only doctor in the *Sonderkommando*. A very sensitive and intelligent man of about thirty-five, Dr Pach had come to Birkenau with a transport from France. His parents, as he told me, had emigrated to France from Poland. He was married in Paris five years earlier, but even his wife's 'Aryan' blood could not save him from deportation. In vain his wife tried to obtain his release from internment. And when with her own eyes she saw him being transported together with many others, she mingled with the crowd of people marked with the Star of David, for she would rather follow the husband she loved into the unknown East than remain behind in the French metropolis, alone and forsaken. However, she had been seen by one of the armed minions and brutally pushed back onto the pavement, away from the 'sub-human scum'.

It was in the spring of 1943 that Jacques Pach was appointed as doctor in the *Sonderkommando*. Here, inside the concentration camp, it was of course impossible for him to find out anything concerning the fate of his beloved wife. If he wanted to go on living he had to abandon all thoughts of her. He felt bitterly lonely and desolate, but he knew there was no cure. And yet Dr Pach was determined to survive. As a medical man he was trained to defend and protect life, including his own, with every means at his disposal. He wore – it seemed a hollow mockery in this environment – a white coat and under it grey riding breeches and brown boots. When I met him for the first time he was commemorating his wedding anniversary. By flickering light of a candle he sat gazing at a photograph of his wife. That he had managed to smuggle this picture into the camp without being caught gave him a certain satisfaction and also great comfort. It was at the invitation of an SS doctor that, after the arrival of his transport, he volunteered for duty at the hospital where supposedly he was to treat wounded soldiers.

Drugs and medicines from almost every European country were stored in a roomy wall cupboard with sliding doors. This hospital was to ensure that sick members of the *Sonderkommando* were treated in isolation. The alternative would have been to take them to the camp hospital where they would have come into contact with other prisoners. In addition to the few drugs and medicines available in the camp there was aspirin, prontosil, bicarb, animal charcoal, opium, luminal, and even sulpha drugs, as well as many other pharmaceutical products which in this place were worth their weight in gold. The people who had brought them here no longer needed them, because Zyclon B gas had cured all their pains and diseases. Thanks to Dr Pach's prudence these drugs not only benefited us but also helped to save the lives of many prisoners in the camp.

Dr Pach's exemplary qualities of humanity stood out against the extreme living conditions prevailing at Birkenau. The way we lived gave only the present any meaning, the past meant nothing and the future not much either. This appalling, detestable and brutal life had already dulled the emotions of many prisoners to such a degree that they were growing more and more indifferent to the crimes which were committed all around them day after day. The camp made people vicious and selfish. Anybody who did not know how to use his elbows sank like a stone. The sight of people suffering, sick, tortured and murdered had become commonplace and scarcely any longer moved anybody. In these surroundings, among spiritually numbed prisoners, it was something out of the ordinary for anyone to help the sick and ailing with selfless dedication as did Dr Pach.

One day Serge, our block senior, was given twenty-five strokes on the buttocks because the SS thought the number of prisoners

reported sick too high. Enraged by the pain Serge flung himself on
Dr Pach and belaboured him with his fists, shouting that he didn't
give a shit for the doctor's kind of medical treatment. 'Listen, you
bloody academic idiot,' he yelled, 'you're not at the Sorbonne
now, you bastard, but in Block 13 at Birkenau. And if you haven't
got the message, you can go and cart stiffs like everybody
else!'

In vain Pach tried to calm the block senior by arguing that it
was not possible to send people to work with pneumonia,
dysentery, typhus or severe burns. What he did not and could not
know, of course, was that to Serge the doctor's little hospital must
have looked like a positive rest home. For, only a year earlier,
Serge had been a corpse bearer in the notorious Block 7 where
prisoners had dropped like flies without anybody taking the
slightest notice. Next morning the Rapportführer went straight to
the sick-bay and checked the number of patients. 'There you are,
that's a bit more like it; told you, didn't I!' he muttered in the
doctor's direction, and walked away satisfied.

A few days later our team was ordered to work in crematorium
3 which from the outside looked exactly like crematorium 2.
However, as I approached the loft I noticed a strong and
disagreeable smell of singeing. I had come to the hair-drying
room. Spread all over the brick floor warmed from the
crematorium ovens below, was women's hair of every colour and
hue, from black through chestnut brown and blonde to grey. The
hair was cut off after the women had been gassed. Washing lines
were strung across the room. Pegged on these lines like wet
washing were further batches of hair which had first been washed
in a solution of ammonium chloride. When the hair was nearly
dry, it was spread on the warm floor to finish off. Finally it was
combed out by prisoners and put into paper bags.

From the thoroughness and care with which SS men checked
that the hair was absolutely dry it was obvious that this was
important material for the war industry. It was not until after the
end of the war that this was confirmed. The hair was used in the
manufacture of industrial felts and threads. Only a few people knew
that fifteen Jewish prisoners were permanently employed in the
crematorium to deal with the raw material. They were all strictly
orthodox Jews ordered to the drying loft by *Kapo* Kaminsky who
wanted to keep them away from the inferno of mass
extermination. Their work was confined to the routine task of

cleaning and drying hair. As orthodox Jews they devoted their entire free time to prayers for the dead and to the study of Jewish religious writings. Their books once belonged to fellow Jews who, like themselves, had believed in the justice of God before they were herded into the gas chambers.

The spiritual leader of this tiny group of orthodox Jews was a man who had been training to become a rabbi. To avoid offending the strict Jewish dietary laws he ate almost nothing but bread, margarine and onions. A tall man of thirty-five with a slight stoop he was put into the *Sonderkommando* shortly after his deportation. But even in the surroundings of a concentration camp he never once lost his faith in God. Because of numerous differences of opinion on matters of faith, he remained here with the group of strictly orthodox Jews, which was small, and clung to him, misunderstood and isolated. Once after the gassing of a transport I witnessed a sharp argument between this group and other prisoners from the *Sonderkommando*. They stuck to their opinion that such an infernal happening could not take place before their eyes if there was really something like a God and a divine justice. 'Listen, Dajan,' said one, 'not once have I felt even a breath of divine justice here. Absolutely everything that you stuffed into my head in school was just nonsense. There is no God, and if there is one, he is an ox and a bastard!' It was 20-year-old Menachem who flung these hard words in his former religious teacher's face.

The scornful laughter of SS myrmidons was always heard when prisoners from the *Sonderkommando* had to burn prayer-books and religious works, and also other books which the Nazis considered degenerate, in a particular oven in crematorium 3. Once when trucks full of books from the belongings store, *Canada*,* were brought in to the crematorium, a couple of prisoners ran to the rabbi in the hair-drying room. They held under his nose religious books that were to be burnt, and said that he must admit that it was naïve to believe any longer in the existence of God. The Dajan tried, using examples from history, to explain to the angry men that as long as mankind had existed, inhumanity like that in Auschwitz had always taken place, even if in a different form, and that everything happening here was really nothing new, but only a repetition of past events. In a choked voice he tried to explain the meaning of the Bible, which not only told the history of the Jews, but was also the expression of an eternal law which stated:

What happened to the fathers is an omen to their descendants. Then a young man called Avroham asked indignantly: 'Dajan, does that mean that the Nazis can commit murder because the Pharaohs committed murder?' Avroham was just twenty-five years old and lived in the Warsaw ghetto – his 20-year-old wife had been slain with their baby. He had then gone to Majdanek, from which he had managed to escape. After wandering for two months near the German–Soviet frontier, he was captured again and brought to Auschwitz. Here he came into the *Sonderkommando*.

'Indeed not,' the Dajan replied almost humbly to Avroham's question. 'I only meant,' he went on, 'that the pious Jew does not read the Bible like a legend, but applies its content to the present. A few years ago when I read in the synagogue from the Book of Esther, which describes the cruel annihilation of the defenceless Jewish people, I had the same feeling as now. When on the eve of the Seder I hear the biblical verses on the more than 300-year-long oppression by the Pharaohs, I experience again the earlier events as our fathers experienced them in the time of the Roman dominion or in the dark days of the Middle Ages. And if the Hagada commands man in each generation to look at himself as if he himself had migrated from Egypt, the brothers who perhaps by a miracle will manage to survive will read the Hagada, made whole by their experiences in Auschwitz, Majdanek or Treblinka. In every generation, my brothers, there were Pharaohs who wanted to exterminate us, but – praise be the Most Holy – he has always rescued us from their hands.' The earnestness and calm with which the Dajan spoke, silenced most of them. Though they did not believe what he had said, most of the assembled prisoners went away more calmed. And not before time, because at that moment *Oberscharführer* Voss came out of crematorium 2 opposite.

The small group of pious people who had congregated round the Dajan were generally treated with respect because they shunned the habits of the place and were not prepared to pay the tribute customary here in order to survive. They had no influence in the *Sonderkommando* for the simple reason that they had nothing to offer for survival but God. And that was not enough.

In 1941 I read in a fascist Slovak daily that the Third Reich no longer needed gold reserves to support its economy, since there was now a new and much fairer system, based on its citizens' enthusiasm for work and far superior to the fraudulent Jewishplutocratic economic system. Two years later the hypocritical mendacity of these phrases was demonstrated before my very eyes.

Towards the end of the summer of 1943 a workshop for melting gold was set up in crematorium 3. It must have been unique in the way in which it obtained its supplies. Two Jewish dental technicians were transferred to Birkenau from the dental hospital in Auschwitz. Their new place of employment was on the groundfloor of crematorium 3. A board outside their door announced *No admission* to prisoners and SS men alike. For it was behind this door that the boxes of gold teeth were opened. These were teeth pulled from the jaws of Jews murdered in the gas chamber before their cremation. The teeth were soaked for a few hours in hydrochloric acid in order to clean off remnants of flesh and bone. Then they were melted in graphite moulds with the help of a blow-lamp and formed into bars. At intervals of about a fortnight the gold was collected by ambulance and taken to Auschwitz. I was told by one of the technicians that frequently they melted down between 5 and 10 kilogrammes a day. After the war it was learned that this gold went into the strong rooms of the *Reichsbank*.

The relative calm at Birkenau in the early days did not last. Soon after my arrival tens of thousands of Jewish citizens from France, Greece, Holland, the ghetto of Bialystok, and the camps of Pomeran, Kola, Zawiercie and Poznan were swallowed up by the insatiable ovens of the crematoria. The liquidation of the ghettos of Sosnovits and Bedzin which began in August 1943 was one of a number of particularly brutal measures carried out in Birkenau at that time. Umpteen thousands were gassed within a period of ten days. This is an account of how it began.

One evening as we marched out on night-shift hundreds of armed SS men were lined up along the street. Because of the comparative closeness of the two towns in Upper Silesia the SS were afraid that the local population as well as the Jews in the ghettos might have come to know about the atrocities perpetrated in Birkenau. For this reason several hundred SS men were ordered to action stations before the start of the campaign.

For some weeks now I had been a stoker in crematorium 5. During this particular night we cremated corpses from a transport from France. The remaining bodies were stacked like logs in the changing room. At dawn next morning all was quiet in the area surrounding the crematorium. The silence was broken by the barking of dogs and the brisk commands of their guards. Preparations were under way for a fresh series of mass murders. Before long we could hear SS men shouting orders. Then came the sound of desperate wailing and lamenting. When I looked out of the window I saw in the grey dawn thousands of people running along the dusty road to the crematorium. On either side SS men struck at them with whips and sticks, kicking them and shouting incessantly: 'Come on, come on, faster, faster!' The column running the gauntlet was several hundred metres long. They ran as fast as they could, but many could not keep up the pace. It was above all the elderly who were left behind. Their sweaty bodies were clad in rags on which the yellow Star of David was sewn. The excited dogs tore not only the people's clothes but snapped at their limbs. Fathers and mothers carrying small children were worst off: they were running for their very lives. Anything encumbering them was dropped on the way, even their last precious piece of bread. Mothers with small children in their arms tried to keep up with their husbands, for they could see what happened to the ones who became winded. Anyone who fell and lay face down in the dust never got up alive.

Presently about 2,000 people were assembled in the crematorium yard. Once they had their breath back, their main concern was for their children. However, before very long they began to realize that what they had gone through was nothing to what awaited them. Facing them was the red-brick building with its two forbidding chimneys belching forth the smoke and the fumes of the fires of hell. They were surrounded by an armed gang of SS men, determined to suppress the least resistance with brutal force. The people were seized by fear and helplessness. Even the children fell silent and no longer asked questions.

Accompanied by his underlings Gorges and Kurschuss, *Oberscharführer* Voss stepped before the crowd and shouted on top of his voice: 'Now listen carefully, you Jews, to what I have to say. In your own interest, I repeat, in your own best interest, I ask you to get undressed as quickly as possible and to put your clothes on the ground by your side .' This unusually terse speech demonstrated one thing: the SS were in no doubt that the people facing them knew exactly what was to befall them. That was why they saved themselves the trouble of talking about the necessity for showers and disinfection and the whole play-acting performance.

A few succinct commands, which said what was required, sufficed.

Standing apart was a group of SS leaders who were obviously watching whether today's method of making short work of the wretched victims would prove feasible. Even *Obersturmführer* Hössler whom, for obvious reasons, we used to call 'Moishe Liar' stood apart and was not called upon to play his usual role.

The effect of the *Oberscharführer*'s request on the people was the same as if they had been told that their lives were finally forfeited. At first sight it seemed that they were resigned to their fate. They began to undress, undressing also their children, and it was as though with every garment they were discarding a little of their lives, those lives which for most of them had, in any case, consisted of nothing but want and privation. Many were fighting back their tears, afraid that their children might be alarmed or start asking questions again. The children, too, were looking around sad-eyed. Quite soon they were all undressed. Husbands and wives embraced, caressing their children and trying to comfort each other. Disappointed with a world that had turned its back on them, they used their last few minutes to search their souls and think about their lives which, however wretched they might have been, still seemed more desirable than the death which now awaited them.

Suddenly from among the crowd a loud voice could be heard: an emaciated little man had begun to recite the Viddui. First he bent forward, then he lifted his head and his arms heavenward and after every sentence, spoken loud and clear, he struck his chest with his fist. Hebrew words echoed round the yard: '*bogati*' (we have sinned), '*gazalti*' (we have done wrong to our fellow men), '*dibarti*' (we have slandered), '*heevetjti*' (we have been deceitful), '*verhirschati*' (we have sinned), '*sadti*' (we have been proud), '*maradti*' (we have been disobedient). 'My God, before ever I was created I signified nothing, and now that I am created I am as if I had not been created. I am dust in life, and how much more so in death. I will praise you everlastingly, Lord, God everlasting, Amen! Amen!' The crowd of 2,000 repeated every word, even though perhaps not all of them understood the meaning of this Old Testament confession. Up to that moment, most of them had managed to control themselves. But now almost everyone was weeping. There were heart-rending scenes among members of families. But their tears were not tears of despair. These people were in a state of deep religious emotion. They had put themselves in God's hands. Strangely enough the SS men present did not intervene, but let the people be.

Meanwhile, *Oberscharführer* Voss stood near by with his cronies, impatiently consulting his watch. The prayers had reached a climax: the crowd was reciting the prayer for the dead which traditionally is said only by surviving relatives for a member of the family who has died. But since after their death there would be nobody left to say the Kaddish for them they, the doomed, recited it while they were still alive. And then they walked into the gas chamber. Zyclon B crystals extinguished their lives while life in the camp and in the *Sonderkommando* went on as usual.

The Jews from the ghettos of Sosnovits and Bedzin had neither hopes nor illusions about their fate in Auschwitz. They lived not far from the camp and knew what to expect.

In the ghettos of Polish towns there were always individuals or small groups who tried to escape. Most of these attempts, undertaken long before the liquidation of these ghettos, came to a tragic end. Members of the Katowice Gestapo used police dogs to unearth the fugitives in their secret hiding-places, mostly in shelters hastily dug in wooded areas, and dragged them out of their burrows like rabbits. Afterwards they were taken to the crematorium at Birkenau where a bullet finished them off. Particularly heart-rending was the sight of young mothers standing naked, their baby in their arms, at the execution wall. Many of these mothers implored their executioners to kill them before their children.

One day I was able to have a last conversation with a small group of Jewish families who had been caught. For four months, so they told me, they lived in dug-outs near Sosnovits, leaving their hiding-places only at night to get a breath of fresh air and also to provide themselves with the bare necessities of life. When their money ran out, their supplies dried up too. Hunger and thirst, cold and disease, took them to the brink of despair. In the end they were given away by the constant crying of their hungry and feverish children. SS patrols who were always prowling around with their dogs tracked them down. Without questioning or trial they were brought to Birkenau from where there was no return. They were exhausted and on the point of collapse, and they knew full well what was in store for them. When the SS men told them to undress they did not seem to take their command in; however, they began to undress slowly.

I was watching a young mother. First she took off her shoes, then the shoes of her small daughter. Then she removed her stockings, then the stockings of the little girl. All the time she endeavoured to answer the child's questions steadily. When she asked: 'Mummy, why are we undressing?' her mother replied: 'Because we must.' When the little girl went on to ask: 'Is the doctor going to examine me, and make me well again?' her sorrowful mother replied: 'He will, my darling, soon you will be well, and then we'll all be happy.' It cost the unfortunate woman all her self-control to utter these words. She was struggling to go on talking to her beloved child quite normally to spare her the terror of her imminent death. In these last few minutes the young mother had aged fifty years. What were her innermost thoughts at this moment? Was she remembering her own youth, her home town, her parents' house or the brief days of her marriage?

At last an SS man came to take her to the place of execution. She lifted up her little girl and hugged her tenderly. She even forgot, so engrossed with her child was she, to bid farewell to her husband who was standing not far from her. And now she stood in front of the wall of execution, holding her child clasped tightly in her arms. The room reeked of fresh, warm human blood. Motionless, her eyes closed, the woman waited for the end; she waited and waited for the killer bullet to take her away from this tormenting life, from this hostile world, into another realm. Did she consider that, as she fell, she might pull her child down and bury it beneath her? That was surely not what she wanted. But neither did she want to be an eyewitness when the life of her darling was extinguished. Meanwhile Voss, the executioner, was circling round mother and child looking for a spot on the child's little body at which to aim his gun. When the distracted mother noticed this she began to twist and turn to the left and to the right, back and forth, anything to take her child out of his field of fire. Suddenly three shots cracked through the silence. The little girl was hit in the side of the chest. Her mother feeling her child's blood flowing down her body lost all self-control and flung her daughter straight at her murderer's head while he was already aiming the barrel of his gun at her. *Oberscharführer* Voss grew very pale and stood there petrified. When he felt the warm blood on his cheek he dropped his gun and wiped his face with his hand. A few seconds went by before *SS-Sturmann* Kurschuss grasped that his chief was no longer master of the situation. Then he hurriedly took hold of Voss' arm. Gorges picked up the murder weapon. 'Carry on, *Rottenführer!*' stammered his unnerved chief, 'I've had enough for today.'

When the execution was over, fifty naked bodies were lying on the ground behind the wall. A few were still breat.::ng stertorously, their limbs moving feebly while they sought to raise their blood-stained heads; their eyes were wide open: the victims were not quite dead because the bullets had missed their mark by a fraction. Gorges went to examine each one and administered the *coup de grace* into the heart or the eye to all who still gave signs of life.

At these executions 6mm small-bore guns were used and fired from a distance of about 3 to 5 centimetres. At the point of entry they left behind a blue-grey stain the size of a silver coin with a small bullet hole in the centre.

Occasionally mentally ill persons were shot in the crematorium. Many accepted death calmly because they did not understand what was happening. In 1943 a few minor transports arrived from Poland, obviously patients from mental hospitals. Conditions there must have been bad, for almost all were under-nourished and emaciated. Their clothes were shabby and threadbare and most of them were crawling with lice. When asked to undress, these people would react in different ways. A few quite clearly did not understand what they were supposed to do; even when the request was repeated with menacing firmness they still stood there impassively. It was only when SS men began to beat and shout at them that they grasped what was expected of them. Many would stare at the SS dazed and frightened only to relapse into complete indifference. Still others marched to and fro muttering incomprehensible monologues, oblivious of what was demanded of them. But then, with them the SS men did not insist on their undressing. As they were led to the wall of death they could see, lying at their feet, their fellow sufferers who had just been shot. Only very few seemed affected by the sight, most just stood there staring vacantly. But there were others who when asked to undress complied with alacrity, giggling and smirking. For often there were females among them, and the thought of seeing naked women excited them intensely.

Among those whom the Gestapo took to the Birkenau crematorium were large numbers of Polish soldiers who had fought as partisans, Russian prisoners of war, and also Polish civilians transferred from prisons. It happened not infrequently that the SS doctor on duty who was required to be present at executions was not immediately available. While we were waiting for him to arrive I occasionally managed to talk to the prisoners. Many of them had been newly arrested, and the majority were strong, well-nourished men in their prime. Not a few had bruises, an indication that they had been beaten or tortured. When asked to undress they realized at once what fate awaited them. Impotence and fear, but also defiance, could be read in their eyes when from the execution room they heard the muffled sounds of shots and the dull thud of falling bodies. But at the last moment even hardened old soldiers and partisans began to tremble. Many shook hands or embraced, others crossed themselves and prayed, although they had not believed in God for a long time. Now, forsaken and with nothing left to cling to, they turned to God and prayed to him.

Five victims at a time were led into the execution room, pushed in front of the wall and held fast. Then, one by one, they were shot in the base of the skull. A few seconds later five dead bodies lay in front of the execution wall. From the bullet wound spurted small fountains of blood. As the corpses were dragged behind the wall the concrete floor swam in blood. Before the next batch of victims was let in the floor was hosed down. Sometimes things became so hectic that we had no time to remove all traces of blood. And then the wretched victims had to stand in the blood of those who had preceded them.

After some time we came to regard anybody arriving at the crematorium as doomed to die. Once the crematorium gate was shut behind them there was no way out and no miracle that could have saved them. It was constant confrontation with atrocities, the thousandfold murders we witnessed daily, and our own impotence to prevent them which led us to adopt this cynical attitude.

At the same time, we of the *Sonderkommando* thought increasingly about ways of freeing ourselves from our seemingly hopeless situation. We realized that we must find allies willing to join us, and we considered people about to go to the gas chamber to be most suitable for this purpose. For their fate was as sealed as ours with the one difference that their liquidation was imminent. They no longer had anything to lose: it is in moments like these that men are determined to do anything and capable of achieving the impossible, the more so when they reckon that there is a chance of survival. It was considerations such as these which led us to believe that, in the face of inexorable and brutal death by gassing, their instinct of self-preservation would make people defend their lives tooth and nail to their dying breath.

So we worked out a plan whereby we would inform members of one of the nocturnal transports of Polish Jews of what awaited them. With their help we would overwhelm the guards and then break out of the crematorium. We thought of Polish Jews because they, having lived inside a ghetto for some time, would have seen and heard things and would therefore be prepared to believe us. Moreover, their Polish mother tongue and their thorough knowledge of the area where, after all, they had grown up, so we reasoned, might help our escape into the mountains. We were firmly determined to put this plan into effect. Our experience so far had taught us that there was no point in suddenly confronting completely ignorant and unsuspecting people with the news that they were about to be gassed without, at the same time, showing them a way out. The effect of such warnings was to put people into a state of fear and panic without a single life being saved.

When in the summer of 1943 a transport arrived from Bialystok a member of the *Sonderkommando* recognized the wife of one of his friends among the arrivals. In the changing room of crematorium 5 he told her quite plainly that they would all be gassed and subsequently cremated. The young woman believed him. After a while, when the full meaning of his ill tidings had sunk in, she began to tremble all over, then she tore her hair, beat her breast and scratched her face with her finger-nails. In a few minutes she had succeeded in disfiguring herself utterly. With her blood-stained face, half-naked, and foaming at the mouth, she ran from one woman to the next, repeating breathlessly what she had learned. What she said sounded so terrible that the women quickly turned away. Since nobody would pay any attention to her she ran across to where the men were undressing. She forced her way through the crowd and cried, her voice shaking: 'Believe me, people, they want to gas and cremate us, do believe me, they are going to gas and cremate us all!' But the men, busy undressing, did not take much notice of her hysterical outburst. Before they had time to listen properly she was already gone. Besides, the way she looked and behaved, her frantic speech, her hasty movements, did nothing to help make her words more credible. She behaved rather like a madwoman so that what she said was not taken seriously. The men went on undressing as if nothing had happened.

However, before very long what the woman had told them began to creep back into people's minds. Reflected in their eyes were fear, uncertainty, disquiet and mistrust. They remembered that in the ghetto they had heard speak of what the woman had told them, even though they could never quite bring themselves to believe it. And the mothers, too, with their small children, now felt instinctively that something was amiss and began, as if by command, to dress first their children and then themselves. When the other women saw this, they did the same. Clearly they felt that in the situation in which they found themselves physical nakedness made them weak and vulnerable.

Meanwhile, SS leaders Schwarzhuber and Hössler were standing by the door of the changing room together with Dr Rhode, the SS doctor on duty. Schwarzhuber was in charge; Hössler's job would be to calm the people – if necessary – with his lies; while Dr Rhode, some time after the poison gas was introduced into the gas chamber, would, by looking through a peep-hole, check that all life inside was extinguished. Only then could the door be opened.

The three SS men were talking together rather animatedly so that they did not immediately notice the tense atmosphere and the alarm among the crowd, Similarly, the other SS men present, Voss, Gorges, Kurschuss, Schillinger and Buntrock, deceived by the people's initial calm behaviour, failed to pay special attention to what went on around them.

The crowd had managed to press forward towards the door. They were all fully dressed and determined to get out of this dangerous building at any price. But where were they to go? To the yard or to the sauna? Or ought they to attempt to escape by forcing their way through the barbed wire? But surely there was no chance of escape here? The building was surrounded by armed SS, determined to shoot anyone trying to escape. Their home was far, so far away. It was not the number of kilometres which separated them from their homes, but simply this world, so alien and so far from their own familiar world that now it existed only in their memory.

The crowd of more than 1,000 kept pressing towards the exit. Suddenly *Oberscharführer* Schillinger who was first to realize what was happening grew deathly pale. He just stood there unable to move: this unexpected situation had caught him completely unawares. The crowd was now only a few metres away from him, but he received no help from his colleagues who had also been taken by surprise. Now the crowd had come face to face with them, while they were still standing there without taking action. They were used to regarding the many who arrived in their daily transports as mere sacrificial lambs. All at once they were faced with a contingency with which they had not reckoned, and it caught them on the hop. They did not look terribly efficient, those hard men. Perhaps they had grown accustomed to regard themselves as more powerful than they actually were.

Lagerführer Schwarzhuber who was standing only a few paces from the exit was the first to react to the threatening attitude of the crowd. With one leap he was outside. His determined action had an electrifying effect on the other SS men. They roused themselves as though from a trance and quickly raced to the door where they formed a chain. They knew that Schwarzhuber would rouse reinforcements which would arrive within a few minutes. Now Hössler, his self-confidence fully restored, stepped forward to face the front row of the pressing throng. He tried to stop the people pressing forward by waving them back. But all his gesticulating and shouting had no effect at all. In desperation he reached into his pocket, drew out a whistle and blew it vigorously several times. The people stopped somewhat puzzled. Slowly the noise died down. The shrill blasts on the whistle had obviously scared them and, at least for the time being, diverted them from their determination to get to the door, come what may.

Fully aware of his initial success, Hössler endeavoured to gain contact with the crowd. 'Now look here, you people,' he said, 'keep calm, in your own interest! Do keep calm!' When he noticed that his words were ignored, he tried once more to attract attention by blowing his whistle. Again he began to speak, this time a little more politely: 'Ladies and gentlemen!'

But before he could go on, the still half-naked woman suddenly popped up before him screaming: 'You want to kill us with gas! I know!'

Immediately Hössler tried to soften the impact of her words. He tapped his forehead and said in a tone clearly intended to ridicule the woman: 'You must be out of your mind, my good woman. Whoever told you that cock-and-bull story?'

'And I do know that you want to kill us with gas, kill us, that's what you want to do, Herr Kommandant!' the woman replied.

Hössler's attempt to undermine the woman's credibility had little effect. The sudden quiet which ensued was a clear indication of the seriousness of the position. The crowd's mistrust grew apace: what the woman had shouted did not seem unbelievable any more; it had had its effect even on the doubters, although they were reluctant to admit it. After all, was it not true that these people came from areas where everybody knew that in Nazi parlance 'resettlement' meant death? And now they realized that they were close to death. How to escape must have been the one thought in all their minds, but escape was there none. They stood there, helpless and confused.

Hössler, sizing up the situation correctly, did some fast talking: 'Ladies and gentlemen!'·he said. 'What in heaven's name has got into you? I've read the *Ortskommandant*'s* report, and according to that the authorities appear to have been quite happy with the behaviour of you Jews in the ghetto. You did your work well and proved that you are good workers. Living conditions here are much better. But in return we do expect discipline. Now just go and get yourselves undressed and ready for your shower. There's no need to be frightened, I give you my word of honour. You are sensible people, aren't you? Surely you're not going to listen to a lunatic? On the other hand, if you don't obey our orders, we'll have to take that as a refusal to work, with serious consequences for you, I'm afraid. Refusing to obey orders really doesn't pay. There's a war on, and everybody must do his or her duty.' While he was speaking Hössler eyed the crowd dispassionately.

During the last few sentences he had to raise his voice because the barking of dogs in the passage almost drowned his words. Then the door was opened. There, flanked by a pack of intimidating dogs, stood SS guards, their pistols in their hands, ready to fire. The dogs were straining at their leads; they were only a few metres away from the crowd and waiting to pounce on them as soon as they were unleashed. They bared their fangs viciously and barked loudly. Some of the children started to cry. Their fathers and mothers lifted them up to comfort them. And now the people understood only too well that all resistance was useless. The show of force on the part of the SS had succeeded: the frightened crowd was willing to do whatever was demanded of them; indeed they would even take that shower if they must, as long as they were given a pledge that they would stay alive.

Once more Hössler addressed them. It would, that was clear from his now unsmiling face, be for the last time. His words were terse and succinct. 'For the last time, do you want to stay alive and work, or are you going on refusing to get undressed?' Slowly the people fell silent. Here and there a dog could be heard barking, children were still sobbing, and a few desperate men and women, on the point of nervous collapse, were weeping noisily. 'Be quiet!' cried Hössler harshly. 'Do be sensible, it is for your own good.' The mood of the people vacillated between disappointment and hope. How gladly they would have abandoned their feelings of fear and mistrust. How happy they would have been if only they could have continued living and working.

And what ought we prisoners to do in this situation? Ought we not to have asked the people to resist and then, together, ended this detestable life honourably? Obsessed by this thought I turned to a fellow prisoner who happened to be standing next to me. He had been an officer in the Greek army and a member of the Resistance. Perhaps he would know what to do. But he was a pragmatist and rejected my suggestion as utterly absurd, arguing that dying heroically and honourably together with our fellows would help no one: we must be patient and bide our time. His words checked my desire for action. I did feel very strongly for the people here, but on reflection I realized the futility of resistance. In my subconscious the feeling that as a passive observer I was guilty had evidently become firmly entrenched. I looked at the SS men and their excited dogs and came back to reality. Of all the places in the whole wide world this must surely be the very one where any attempt at saving human lives was a senseless undertaking.

For a brief minute or two the people stood hesitating and not knowing what to do. But there was the SS, there were the dogs growling and barking, and the crowd knew they must submit. One by one they turned away; slowly they began to undress again. Who can tell whether they may not still, even now, have clung to a last, a very last hope that a miracle might happen. For death is always inconceivable.

They died in the gas chamber not long afterwards, cheated of their hope for a miracle. The only one who stayed alive a few hours longer was the woman who had wanted to warn the others. She was taken to a room next to the gas chamber where she was interrogated under torture. Making her talk was not difficult for the SS who had plenty of experience in such matters. Every prisoner working in the crematorium was lined up for an identity parade. And sure enough it was not long before the woman identified the man who had told her that they were all to be gassed and cremated.

While the woman was being shot, SS men bound the prisoner. Then Voss and Kurschuss led him to one of the ovens. He was pushed inside and burnt alive. The rest of us were made to watch his hideous end. Obviously the SS meant to set an example. Nevertheless there was another incident a few months later when a friend of mine met a similar gruesome death for telling people from the camp of Westerbork that they were to be gassed.

But there were also Jews who lived so far away from Auschwitz that they had not the least premonition of the fate that awaited them here. About 500 kilometres north-west of Athens lies the town of Salonika. Before World War 2 it had been one of Greece's important agricultural and commercial centres. Since the spring of 1943 a large number of transports of Jews from there arrived in Auschwitz. Almost all of them died in the gas chambers. Their journey took more than seven days and seven nights crammed in cattle trucks, without sufficient food and, worse still, water. Many died during the journey. By the time they arrived in Birkenau they had undergone incredible hardships. Although their supplies of milk had almost dried up, the mothers tried hard to breast-feed their babies. As for the aged and the sick, anyone could see that they were at the end of their tether.

Obersturmführer Hössler decided to have a field-day that summer morning some thousand innocent, unsuspecting people arrived from Salonika. Once again this arch liar, had thought up a plan of how to torment and hoodwink a starving and parched crowd. His carefully prepared address went something like this: 'On behalf of the camp administration I bid you welcome. This is not a holiday resort but a labour camp. Just as our soldiers risk their lives at the front to gain victory for the Third Reich, you will have to work here for the welfare of a new Europe. How you tackle this task is entirely up to you. The chance is there for every one of you. We shall look after your health, and we shall also offer you well-paid work. After the war we shall assess everyone according to his merits and treat him accordingly. Now, would you please all get undressed. Hang your clothes on the hooks we have provided and please remember your number. When you've had your bath there will be a bowl of soup and coffee or tea for all. Oh yes, before I forget, after your bath, please have ready your indentures, diplomas, school reports and any other documents so that we can employ everybody according to his or her training and ability. Would diabetics who are not allowed sugar report to staff on duty after their baths.'

Hössler's respectable appearance and the genuineness of his words – which an *SS-Unterführer* translated into Greek – had a reassuring and stimulating effect on the weary crowd. Many felt a flicker of hope, but many others grew thoughtful. To them there seemed to be a discrepancy between the SS leader's promises and their experiences during the transport. Why, if they were urgently needed here, were they given no drinking water during their journey, and why were so many allowed to die? On the other hand, not one of them could have envisaged that a few hours later they would all have been transformed into a handful of ashes. What rational grounds were there for transporting more than 1,000 people from Salonika to Birkenau only to murder them? Surely it would have been simpler to do away with them in Greece? And besides, it was, after all, wartime and the Germans had urgent need of each and every railway engine and truck in order to transport their war materials to the wastes of Russia.

When Hössler had finished his address, the people began to undress, the men on one side, women and children on the other. Still plagued by hunger and thirst and remembering that food and drink had been promised them after their baths they now pushed and shoved to be first in the 'showers'. Thus, a towel slung over their arm and clutching a cake of soap, they entered, all unsuspecting, the three gas chambers of crematorium 5.

From the Red Cross ambulance which had accompanied the transport up to the crematorium, two SS men took the so-called disinfectants, several canisters of Zyclon B and poured their contents into the openings above the gas chamber. All they required to carry out this task, in addition to the conviction that they were serving their fatherland, was a hammer, a tin opener and a gas-mask.

One evening towards the end of October I went on night duty as one of a team of 100 prisoners. Together with another few experienced prisoners I was picked for this team by *Kapo* Kaminsky and instructed to *organize* valuables, if possible. We needed them urgently to buy weapons which, in Auschwitz, could be bought for vast sums from the salvage yards. During the salvaging of aircraft wrecks and other damaged war material the prisoners working there occasionally managed to find usable arms and munitions which they sold for gold, dollars or diamonds. Money and valuables were also needed to support escape plans and to bribe SS men.

We, the prisoners of the *Sonderkommando*, kept thinking about how we might make public to the world details of the gruesome crimes which were perpetrated here. We believed that thereby a stop might be put to the mass murders. A prisoner who had witnessed the fearful crimes committed daily in the camp would be most suited to this task: therefore one of them must be helped to escape.

Bribing SS men was no less important. They were intensely attracted by gold, dollars and diamonds. With the help of these commodities it was possible to keep many of them from what they regarded as the execution of their duty. Furthermore, once an SS man had accepted gold or diamonds *organized* by prisoners, he was faced with a number of problems. For he had contravened orders and if found out or given away must expect severe punishment. He had also in a way become dependent on us prisoners. Then again, he must find safe hiding-places for his valuables; and finally there was the worry of whether he would manage to get his ill-gotten treasures safely home.

This evening as I went on night duty the crematorium yard was deserted, dimly and scantily lit by a few arc lamps. From afar we could hear the sound of women's voices. They came from the women's camp which was separated from crematorium 2 only by a fence. No doubt this was the hour when the famished inmates were given their daily bread rations. Every oven had been fired since morning. We were ordered to keep the fires going which meant feeding them with two wheelbarrowfuls of coke every half hour.

Contrary to their wont, several SS leaders including *Oberscharführer* Voss and his aides, Gorges, Kurschuss and Ackermann were in the crematorium before us, busily dashing about and poking their noses into all sorts of things. They checked to see that the fire in the ovens was burning well; they checked the door to the mortuary to make sure it was properly locked; they checked that there were no traces of blood anywhere; they checked the fans; and they switched the light in the gas chamber on and off a few times. Normally the concrete floors in the gas chamber as well as in the changing room were damp: today they were carefully dried. To this end a few coke-burning stoves had been set up and kept going all day. Kurschuss was running about holding a large atomizer from which he sprayed clouds of a sweetish fragrance. Quite obviously the people expected today must not be met by the customary musty odour, but rather get the impression that they were in fact inside a perfectly hygienic bath-house. The notices at the entrance to the changing room were replaced by new and larger ones. The red letters announcing that this was the 'entrance to the baths and disinfecting room' stood out well against a pale blue background.

Another party of *SS-Unterführers* arrived, among them Quackernack, Hustek, Emmerich, Schillinger and *Obersturmführer* Schwarzhuber, together with Dr Thilo, medical officer on duty. All was now ready to receive this clearly out-of-the-ordinary transport.

After a while a convoy of trucks covered with tarpaulins entered the crematorium yard. The SS men who had come with the transport leapt down from the running-boards, ran to the back and let down the tail-boards. Then they raised the tarpaulins and asked the people to step down. This was done so courteously that I could hardly believe my eyes and ears. I was puzzled: what sort of people were these who had just arrived? I noticed that not one of them wore a Star of David. As the people were climbing down from the trucks there was none of the usual shouting, beating and general harassment. On the contrary, the SS men were at their most polite and helpful wherever required. After a short while some 1,000 people were standing in the yard. There were more men than women; all were well dressed, none had any luggage; that, too, was unusual.

A wooden box was set up in the centre of the yard arousing the interest of the people who craned their necks to see what was going on. Climbing onto this improvised speaker's platform was *Lagerführer* Schwarzhuber, followed by a man in a leather coat and grey hat with the brim pulled well down. I thought he might be a member of the Gestapo who had been assigned to a special mission. In the yard all was hushed. The crowd stood expectantly, waiting to be addressed.

Schwarzhuber spoke first: 'Ladies and gentlemen!' he began. 'On behalf of the camp administration I welcome you. We have been instructed to do everything possible to expedite your departure abroad. For this purpose a representative of the Foreign Ministry is here to tell you how the rest of your journey has been organized, and he will now speak to you.'

The so-called representative of the Foreign Ministry now mounted the platform. 'Ladies and gentlemen!' he said. 'I have been instructed by the Foreign Ministry to organize your journey to Switzerland. This is your last stop on the territory of the Third Reich. We have brought you here because the Swiss authorities insist that each one of you must be disinfected before you cross the frontier.' He went on officiously: 'Here we have the facilities for carrying out large-scale disinfection proceedings. In this building,' he pointed at the crematorium, 'a large bath-house has been installed where you are to go later. Another thing! After your bath, please have your travel documents ready so that we can certify that you have been disinfected. Once more, may I point out that the Swiss authorities have declared that nobody will be allowed to cross the frontier without this certificate in his passport. Your special train is waiting at the station. It is scheduled to depart at 7 tomorrow morning and will take you to the frontier. I would therefore ask you in your own interest to follow the instructions of the camp personnel. May I end by wishing you a pleasant journey for tomorrow.'

It seemed to me that these words had the desired effect. Instinctively many people reached into their breast pockets as though to make sure that their passports were still there. For at that moment they meant more to them than anything else in the world.

The way in which the so-called representative of the Foreign Ministry behaved, his gestures and, above all, his voice, seemed familiar. He was indeed none other than *Obersturmführer* Hössler.

Not long after Hössler's address all the people had left for the underground changing room. Hössler's promises and the courteous and correct conduct of the SS men helped to make everything go off without a hitch. We prisoners of the *Sonderkommando* were kept away. Perhaps they thought that our presence might make the people hesitant or give us a chance of speaking to them.

The order for the *Kapo* of the stoker team to fill up the ovens with coke came about a quarter of an hour later than usual. No doubt the delay had been carefully planned: first, it was necessary to wait until the yard had been cleared of people; and second, the noise of coke being fed into the ovens might have made the crowd suspicious.

The lift linking the underground rooms with the cremation room was constantly going up and down. The nervousness displayed by the SS men indicated that, after initially all going so perfectly according to plan, their well-organized murder operation had struck a snag. Kaminski, our *Kapo*, was ordered to stand by with eighteen prisoners, of whom I was one. Some time later an SS man took us down in the lift. There we waited in the corridor from which doors led to the gas chamber, the mortuary, and the changing room. From the latter came a humming of voices, and, at intervals, firm commands ordering the people to undress.

Eventually *Oberscharführer* Voss took us into the mortuary. There behind a pile of emaciated corpses six hand-painted signboards were propped against the wall. They had the letters A–D, E–H, and so on, down to Z, painted on them in black letters and had arrived at the crematorium some days earlier; nobody could imagine what they were meant for. And now the mystery was to be resolved. *Oberscharführer* Voss lined us up in rows of three. The man in the middle of each row was told to hold one of the boards. Then we marched into the changing room where we took our places along one of the walls, facing the people who had come with the transport. Each board was turned so that they could read the letters.

Naturally we attracted their attention and suddenly there was a silence while the crowd was looking at us and at the boards. Hössler, that cunning fox, who was still playing his part as representative of the Foreign Ministry, swiftly exploited the silence. He stepped before the crowd and started to speak again: 'Ladies and gentlemen!' he began. 'You can all see the boards with the letters of the alphabet which have just been brought in. Now please look at them carefully.' Here he pointed at the boards, one after the other, from A to Z. Then he went on: 'When you have dressed after your bath, kindly queue up at the board with the first letter of your surname where you will be given a certificate confirming that you have been disinfected. Please also remember the number of your hook in the changing room so that the necessary formalities can be dealt with as quickly and as smoothly as possible. And do not regard this disinfection business as something we have thought up to annoy you. It is, let me re-emphasize, the Swiss authorities who insist on it. It is therefore in your own interest to submit to this unavoidable procedure as quickly as possible. You must also remember that railway tracks are often blocked through enemy terror raids. So please hurry up if you want to get away from here without delay!' While he was finishing his speech Hössler gazed at the people facing him like a priest eager to gain the confidence and credibility of his congregation.

When he had finished, the people went into huddles to consult each other. They were talking in Yiddish, and some of them had clearly become suspicious. They were Jews from eastern Europe who doubtless had heard rumours of mass extermination. And yet Hössler's words had impressed many so that they now began to undress. But there were others who were still standing around undecided, ignoring the constant urgings by the SS men that they should hurry and undress. Hössler's speech had not convinced them. They knew somehow that they were in a trap and that their lives were at risk. Therefore they thought it best not to take off their clothes which contained their travel documents.

After a few minutes' hesitation the SS men began to usher the ones who had undressed into the gas chamber, possibly in the belief that once they had them out of the way they might be able to deal with the recalcitrant ones more efficiently.

Presently more than half the people were behind the great door of the gas chamber. It seemed that the others still in the changing room were trying to gain time. Time for what, though? The crematorium was surrounded by armed SS men. None of us prisoners was willing to join them in what would be a senseless attempt to get away. Nor was there any chance of telling the people that they were about to be gassed. This might have persuaded them that it was more honourable to die fighting than meekly inside the gas chamber. However, every phase, from their arrival on the ramp to the moment when they were hustled into the gas chamber was deliberately carried out in a tearing hurry leaving the victims no time to think or take decisions.

Surreptitiously *SS-Unterführer*s Quackernack, Hustek, Voss, Boger, Schillinger, Gorges, Emmerich, Kurschuss, Ackermann and others left the changing room one by one, returning after a short time armed with sticks. No doubt *Lagerführer* Schwarzhuber had given them the green light to deal with these people in the usual way. Instead of their earlier marked courtesy and lying talk

there were now terse requests of 'Get undressed! Hurry up! Get
ready for your baths! Come on, come on!' The people did not
respond, but simply kept standing about, doing nothing. It was
not surprising therefore that the SS men grew nervous. In order to
demonstrate that they meant business they shifted their holsters
round to the front and opened the flaps. Then they came closer to
the crowd and, assuming a menacing attitude, began to shout.
When this had no effect either, they started to strike blindly at the
crowd with their sticks. Now the ones standing in front, in an
attempt to dodge the blows, tried to back away while those
exposed in turn tried to get out of the way, so that there was utter
chaos. The SS increased their furious, merciless beatings. By now
many people were bleeding profusely from blows they had
received. And at long last the rest realized that resistance was
useless. There was no way out. They began to undress, whereupon
the SS men stopped beating them. Why we were still standing by
the wall holding our boards no one knew.

It was obvious that the SS felt themselves once more to be
masters of the situation. Quackernack and Schillinger were
strutting back and forth in front of the humiliated crowd with a
self-important swagger. Suddenly they stopped in their tracks,
attracted by a strikingly handsome woman with blue-black hair
who was taking off her right shoe. The woman, as soon as she
noticed that the two men were ogling her, launched into what
appeared to be a titillating and seductive strip-tease act. She lifted
her skirt to allow a glimpse of thigh and suspender. Slowly she
undid her stocking and peeled it off her foot. From out of the
corner of her eye she carefully observed what was going on round
her. The two SS men were fascinated by her performance and paid
no attention to anything else. They were standing there with arms
akimbo, their whips dangling from their wrists, and their eyes
firmly glued on the woman.

She had taken off her blouse and was standing in front of her
lecherous audience in her brassiere. Then she steadied herself
against a concrete pillar with her left arm and bent down, slightly
lifting her foot, in order to take off her shoe. What happened next
took place with lightning speed: quick as a flash she grabbed her
shoe and slammed its high heel violently against Quackernack's
forehead. He winced with pain and covered his face with both
hands. At this moment the young woman flung herself at him and
made a quick grab for his pistol. Then there was a shot. Schillinger

cried out and fell to the ground. Seconds later there was a second shot aimed at Quackernack which narrowly missed him.

A panic broke out in the changing room. The young woman had disappeared in the crowd. Any moment she might appear somewhere else and aim her pistol at another of her executioners. The SS men realized this danger. One by one they crept outside. The wounded Schillinger was still lying unattended on the floor.

After a while a few SS men came in and dragged him hastily to the door. Then a third shot was fired: one of the SS men pulling Schillinger let go of him and started to limp to the door as fast as he could. Then the light went out. Simultaneously the door was bolted from the outside. We, too, were now caught inside the pitch-dark room.

The people who had lost their bearings in the dark were running about in confusion. I, too, was afraid that this might be the end for all of us. Just now, I thought ruefully, when our plans for a rebellion were going ahead, and when we had a not inconsiderable hoard of arms and ammunition, why did it have to be just now? I began to grope my way along the wall towards the exit. When I finally reached it I found nearly all of my companions, but also many of the others who instinctively had made for the door. They were weeping and bemoaning their fate, some were praying, others bidding each other farewell. There was considerable speculation as to the identity of the woman who had fired the shots.

A man who was standing near us had noticed that we did not belong to their group. He spoke to us in the dark and wanted to know from where we came.

'From the death factory,' one of my companions replied tersely.

The man was very agitated and demanded loudly: 'I don't understand what this is all about. After all, we have valid entry visas for Paraguay; and what's more, we paid the Gestapo a great deal of money to get our exit permits. I handed over three diamonds worth at least 100,000 zloty; it was all I had left of my inheritance. And that young dancer, the one who fired the shots a little while ago, she had to pay a lot more.'

Suddenly the door was flung open. I was blinded by the glare of several searchlights. Then I heard Voss shouting: 'All members of the *Sonderkommando*, come out!' Greatly relieved we dashed outside and ran up the stairs and into the yard. Outside the door to the changing room two machine-guns had been set up, and behind them several searchlights. Steel-helmeted SS men were lying ready to operate the machine-guns. A horde of armed SS men were milling about in the yard.

I was on my way to the cremation room when a car drew up and *Lagerkommandant* Höss climbed out. Then there was the rattle of machine-guns. A terrible blood-bath was wrought about the people caught in the changing room. A very few who had managed to hide behind pillars or in corners were later seized and shot. In the meantime, the 'disinfecting officers' had thrown their deadly Zyclon B gas down into the gas chamber where the credulous, placing their trust in Hössler's deceitful words, had gone less than an hour earlier.

Next morning we learnt that Schillinger had died on the way to hospital, while *Unterscharführer* Emmerich had been wounded. The news was received with satisfaction by many camp inmates; for in section B2d of the men's camp Schillinger had been regarded as an extremely brutal and capricious sadist.

The body of the young dancer was laid out in the dissecting room of crematorium 2. SS men went there to look at her corpse before its incineration. Perhaps the sight of her was to be a warning as well as an illustration of the dire consequences one moment's lack of vigilance might have for an SS man.

As for us, these events had taught us once again that there simply was no chance of escape once a person entered the crematorium: by then it was too late. The promises of the SS, ranging from work inside the camp to emigration to Switzerland, were nothing but barefaced deception, as they had proved to be for these wretched people who had wanted to emigrate to Paraguay.

Chapter 4
The tragedy of the
Family Camp

The Allied advance at the war fronts failed to halt the process of mass extermination. On the contrary, more and more Jews from all over Europe were deported to Auschwitz, many of them to perish immediately after their arrivals in the gas chambers of Birkenau.

In February 1944 there was a selection* among members of the *Sonderkommando*. One evening during roll-call *Lagerführer* Schwarzhuber, *Rapportführer* Polotschek and another few SS men appeared in the yard of Block 13. From among the prisoners they selected about 200, telling them that they would be transferred to Lublin where strong men were needed for a special job. Most of them belonged to the group which, with Hössler in charge, had taken part in removing all traces of the mass graves near bunkers 1 and 2. Since work there had come to an end, they were now expendable.

Less than three months later we learnt what had happened to them in Lublin. In April 1944, nineteen Russian prisoners of war with their German *Kapo*, arrived in Birkenau from Lublin where they had been working in the *Sonderkommando*. The concentration camp of Lublin was evacuated because the advancing Red Army was dangerously near. Even before we had a chance of talking to one of the Russians, we realized what had happened to our team-mates; several of the newcomers wore clothing and boots which had belonged to the *Kapos* and foremen in our group. There was no mistaking the blue jackets and the made-to-measure boots. We were informed later that in February about 200 prisoners had arrived in Lublin and had been gassed immediately. The Russian prisoners of war had spoken to some of them in the changing room and had been told that they were from Birkenau where they had worked in the *Sonderkommando*.

This selection in February 1944 caused wide-spread alarm among us prisoners. Although the brisk advance of the Red Army raised new hopes in the hearts of many camp inmates, members of the *Sonderkommando* no longer seriously believed that they would live to see the liberation. It stood to reason that the perpetrators of daily mass murders would not allow a single witness of their crimes to stay alive and to testify against them. We had therefore come to the conviction that only a mass escape could save us.

Time was running out, but how were we to organize an escape? True, we owned three hand-grenades. We also had a few semi-automatic revolvers and 6.35mm pistols plus ammunition which we had *organized* for vast sums of money from the prisoners in the dismantling shops.

In the dangerous situation in which we found ourselves it seemed important to convince as many prisoners in the camp as possible of the necessity to rise up and to invite them to join us. This was not easy because so far their lives were not directly threatened while their chance of survival appeared to increase with every day that passed. For us in the *Sonderkommando* it was exactly the opposite. The Resistance in the camp fully understood our impatience to strike but considered the time had not yet come. Therefore our people were told to wait for the weather to improve and the front to move still nearer; for then the partisans, large numbers of whom were said to be hiding close to the camp, would be able to support our uprising. But arrangements would have to be made with them beforehand.

Despite this delay, inside the *Sonderkommando* plans for a break-out were continually discussed and stepped up. Our leaders were experienced, level-headed and fearless men. At first they thought that it would be best if only the strongest and boldest were to take part in the uprising. But gradually they became convinced that it would be better if everybody were to join in, each one being given a special task. Although we all realized that only a lucky few would succeed in escaping, everybody was to have a real chance. Many were helped by this faint glimmer of hope to regain their lost self-respect and self-confidence and to give new meaning to their life.

We had still not recovered from the fright of the February selection when we suffered another blow. One day one of our

Kapos called Vladek who had worked as a stoker in the old Auschwitz crematorium before I arrived, was taken away and locked up in a bunker cell in Block 11. The SS men of the political department thought that, as he was a former official of the Polish Communist Party, they might extract from him important information concerning the organization and personnel structure of the Polish underground movement. For months he was interrogated and tortured, but he remained steadfast and never gave away a single name. When they realized that they could not make him talk, he was returned to the *Sonderkommando*.

Vladek was about twenty-eight, blond and stocky, intelligent, unafraid, and very experienced in organizing conspiracies. All of us in the *Sonderkommando* respected and valued him as a reliable fellow prisoner.

When the Germans occupied Warsaw he joined the underground until he was arrested. Now he was one of the leading figures of the Resistance group in the *Sonderkommando*; he played a prominent part in planning the uprising as well as acting as go-between with the Resistance in the camp. Since, like the rest of the Polish prisoners, he was quartered in Block 2, he could move freely in camp B2d. Moreover, there was a genuine bond of friendship between him and most of the Polish political prisoners who played important parts in the Resistance movement. Vladek was among those in the *Sonderkommando* who were vigorously pressing for a break-out because he felt his own life to be particularly threatened. One day, for no obvious reason, he was transferred back to Auschwitz. This did not bode well. Not a week had gone by when one afternoon an ambulance arrived in the crematorium yard. *Oberscharführer* Quackernack jumped out and went inside the *Kommandoführer*'s office where Gorges happened to be working. A little later Gorges walked into the cremation room and ordered a couple of stokers to go outside with Quackernack. Presently they returned carrying a sack which was tied up. Quite obviously it contained a corpse whose identity was to be kept secret. Quackernack was rather nervous and snapped at us to burn the sack at once. However, we had difficulties in putting the sack right inside the oven. Then, as we were winding down the door, a corner of the sack was caught so that we had to wind it up again to release the sack and push it right inside. Meanwhile the sacking had been almost completely destroyed by the flames exposing what it was meant to conceal. Anybody standing close by was able to recognize the corpse as that of Vladek. Accounts of the incident spread like wildfire.

There were a few radicals who more than once had wanted to strike off on their own. Now they renewed their violent criticism of the leaders of the Resistance. They reproached them with irresponsibly postponing the uprising, holding them responsible not only for the death of several of their comrades who had been gassed a few weeks earlier in Majdanek, but also for Vladek's fate.

One evening towards the end of February I was on night-shift. When our team arrived at crematorium 5 a few hundred corpses were lying in the changing room waiting to be cremated. In the *Kommandoführer*'s office, which was connected with the cremation room by a door, a party was in full swing. *Kommandoführer* Johann Gorges had been promoted from *Rottenführer* to *Unterscharführer*, and it was he who had organized this festivity.

Gorges was about forty, six feet tall, of robust build and clumsy gait. His face was always flushed – earning him the nickname of Moische Borak, 'beetroot face' – and his hair cropped short like an army recruit's. He seemed almost totally devoid of feelings. When he was present at executions he registered neither satisfaction nor pity. Although he carried out his orders obediently he never did more than he had been bidden, neither did he indulge in sadistic tortures. No doubt he would have led a dully normal and uneventful life, had not fate taken him to Auschwitz as a member of the SS. He drank a great deal, mostly the hard stuff. When he had a skinful he used to grow talkative, even with us. Then he would go on about his son of whom he was inordinately proud. Often he raved about France, especially about Paris, where he seemed to have spent happier days. Between him and us stokers there was a strange, almost human, relationship born out of close proximity and nights spent in each other's company in the crematorium.

This particular night I was exempt from oven duty because I had been detailed for duty as odd-job man. This involved cleaning the *Kommandoführer*'s office, polishing the boots of SS men on duty, seeing to the stove in the passage and washing the dishes. However, I did not have the quiet night to which I had been looking forward. The long table in the *Kommandoführer*'s office was spread with delicacies from all over the world. There were tinned foods, cold meats, cheese, olives, sardines, and other dainties, all taken, needless to say, from deportees. There was also Polish vodka to wash them down and ample supplies of cigarettes. About a dozen *SS-Unterführer*'s had come to the crematorium to celebrate Gorges' promotion. They sat round the table eating and drinking. One of them had brought his accordion and was playing folk and pop songs with the others joining in. They told each other blue jokes, and as the hour advanced the mood grew increasingly genial. Once Gorges was sufficiently sloshed, he began boasting of how he took part in a parade in Paris. Jumping up from his chair he goose-stepped round the table, saluting and bawling marching music.

From the cremation chamber came the noise of fans humming, *Kapos* shouting and stokers stoking the corpses inside the ovens with their iron forks.

The banquet lasted until midnight. One after the other the guests, all of them rather drunk, left. Gorges was the last to go. After they had gone the air in the room reeked of booze and stale cigarette smoke. I opened the window to let in some fresh air and began clearing the table. *Oberscharführer* Voss had been one of the guests at Gorges' party. That night he was on crematorium duty and had gone to check that everything was all right. When he returned he took off his jacket and boots, lay down on a straw mattress and fell asleep at once.

I was busy cleaning his boots when I heard the noise of a motor cycle approaching. The machine stopped outside the crematorium. I managed, with difficulty, to rouse Voss from his slumber, and he was only just coming round when the door opened and *Oberscharführer* Hustek of the political department came in. They saluted; Hustek handed Voss a sealed envelope; there was a brief exchange of words; then Hustek departed on his motor cycle.

As a rule Hustek was the bringer of ill tidings. Whenever he appeared in the crematorium a major extermination campaign was imminent; that was why we in the *Sonderkommando* called him Malchemowes, 'Angel of death'. Hustek was forty, but because his face was cross-hatched with lines and wrinkles he looked much older. He had the reputation of being brutal and violent and everybody gave him a wide berth if they could.

After Hustek's departure, Voss sat down at the table to read the message. While he was scanning it he indignantly shook his head a few times. He was quite clearly furious, and when he had finished he flung the letter down on the table shouting irritably: 'Jesus bloody Christ! It can't be done by tomorrow morning, it needs more time. This is too much! It's always me that has to see to everything. Voss, Voss, Voss, that's all *I* ever hear! I can work my fingers to the bone in this place, that's all right, but the minute there's a hitch, I cop it!' Only then did he realize that I was still there. 'Go and get the *Kapo*s! At the double!' he barked. I ran as fast as I could to the cremation room to call the two *Kapo*s, Sehlojme and Vacek.

It was a longish room, perhaps 160 square metres in area, and it was shrouded in acrid smoke and fumes. In the middle stood two big rectangular oven complexes, each of which had four burning chambers. Between the ovens were the generators which lit the fire and kept it going. The coke fuel was brought in in wheelbarrows. The raging flames rushed into the open air through two underground conduits which connected the ovens with the massive chimneys. The force and heat of the flames were so great that the whole room rumbled and trembled. A couple of sweaty, soot-blackened prisoners armed with metal scrapers fitted with wooden handles were busy raking out a whitish glowing substance from the bottom of one of the ovens. It had gathered in grooves which were let into the concrete floor under the flux-holes of the oven. When it had cooled somewhat it was grey-white. It was the ashes of human beings who had been alive yesterday and had left the world after an agonizing martyrdom, without anyone taking any notice.

While the ash was being raked out of one lot of ovens, the ventilators of the one next to it were being switched on and the preparations made for a new batch. Indeed a largish number of corpses were lying on the wet concrete floor. They had already undergone the usual treatment: gold teeth had been broken out and the women's hair cut off.

In front of each oven lay a metal trough, in the front of and under which a squared timber had been pushed diagonally, and behind there were two poles like those of a stretcher. As always, a bucket of water was poured over the trough first, then two prisoners laid three corpses on it while, with a loud rattling, the oven door was cranked up like a metal curtain. One in front and one behind, pairs of prisoners lifted up the stretcher and put it on the rollers in front of the entrance, and pushed it into the oven. When it was pulled out an iron fork was pushed against the corpses so that they stayed inside the oven. When the oven door had been cranked down again the cremation began. This was the customary picture which met my eyes that night when I entered the cremation room to call the *Kapo*s. The noise and din were so great that I could hardly make out my own words. I yelled to the two men as loudly as I could, and gave them to understand that they were to report to Voss. Then I went back to the *Kommandoführer*'s office.

Standing to attention in front of Voss they waited for his orders. He demanded to know how many corpses there were still uncremated in the mortuary. One of the *Kapo*'s replied that it was difficult to say exactly how many, but there might be 450 or 500. 'What do you mean, might be?' shouted Voss in a temper. 'I want to know precisely how many there are.' He glared at the second *Kapo* who shrugged his shoulders. Voss nearly burst a blood vessel: 'You are a couple of fucking useless bastards! Do I have to worry about that sort of thing as well?' He stood up and rushed into the changing room, the two *Kapo*s trailing close behind.

Meanwhile I remained in the *Kommandoführer*'s office. Carefully, I closed the door, having first made sure that the coast was clear. Then I hurried to the table and with shaking hands picked up the sheet of paper and hastily read it. Its content made my blood run cold. When Voss returned with the two *Kapo*s I had difficulty in not giving myself away.

Voss sat down and lit a cigarette. Then he muttered: 'Hm, it might well be that there are still 500 to be processed.' Then he took the letter and pushed it carelessly into the pocket of his uniform jacket. While he sat staring in front of him he was probably turning over in his mind the problem of how to get rid of the 500-odd corpses in the mortuary by the following morning. For according to the secret order which I had read, crematorium 5 was to be ready as from 8 a.m. to deal with the gassing of the inmates of the Family Camp.

The Family Camp was set up in September 1943 when about 5,000 Jews arriving from Theresienstadt were quartered in camp B2b. Later transports from Theresienstadt also went into the Family Camp.

When in the year 1784 the Emperor Francis Joseph of Austria named the fortress after his mother, the Empress Maria Theresa, he little suspected the purpose for which it was to be used 157 years later. The fortress, sited where the river Eger flows into the Elbe, had been built as a defence against renewed attacks from Prussia.

At the time of the Habsburg monarchy the forward citadel, known as the small fortress, had already become a notorious prison. It was here that Gavrilo Princip died, the Bosnian student whose assassination of Archduke Francis Ferdinand, heir to the Austrian throne, triggered off World War 1.

In the first Republic of Czechoslovakia Theresienstadt, now Terezin, remained a garrison town. But after the occupation of Bohemia and Moravia by the Germans, all inhabitants were compulsorily resettled, while the town which is surrounded by wide ramparts became a ghetto for Jews from Bohemia, Moravia, Germany, Austria, and later also from Holland. From the autumn of 1941 an increasing number of Jews were quartered in the depopulated residential districts as well as in the roomy barracks of Theresienstadt. They provided a reservoir for the places of extermination which had been established further east, and very few of them survived the Third Reich. The little fortress, on the other hand, was used as a prison for political prisoners.

In September 1943 a few thousand Jews were deported from Theresienstadt to Auschwitz and put in the camp without the usual selection on the ramp. To us older prisoners this seemed almost unbelievable. Still more unbelievable was the fact that behind the barbed wire of their camp the detainees did not wear prison garb but were allowed civilian clothes. They did not even have their hair shaved off. Compared to the rest of the camp inmates their physical and mental condition was relatively good.

Nobody could find a valid reason why it was these Jews from Theresienstadt had been spared the walk to the gas chamber, or why their living conditions were incomparably better than those of the other prisoners. They were made to do the work of building their own camp, but they were never used as forced labour. Every month they were allowed to write one post-card and receive one parcel from outside. Pregnant women and babies were given small quantities of milk, butter and even white bread. Children under six went to a nursery school, while the older children were taught by Jewish teachers. In the Family Camp there existed an excellent orchestra among whose members were well-known artists, and which on occasions had to perform before the SS. There was even a hospital where noted university professors and doctors worked, and all this in a place where, not 100 metres away, a human life was worth nothing. It was, therefore, not surprising that these unusual conditions led us to assume that the Family

Camp was under the special protection of the International Red Cross. However, the secret order which I had read that night showed me that this was not so. It was more likely that the Jews in the Family Camp were used to provide an alibi for the Nazis, to demonstrate to the world how well they treated the Jews in concentration camps, and that this was the reason why they had been given special status.

Voss was still sitting at the table, thoughtfully drumming the table top with his pencil and consulting his wrist-watch; then he began scribbling figures on a scrap of paper. After a while he turned to the *Kapos* and said: 'To get the stiffs burnt by tomorrow morning is no problem. All you have to do is to see that every other load consists of two men and one woman from the transport, together with a *Mussulman* and a child. For every other load use only good material from the transport, two men, one woman and a child. After every two loadings empty out the ashes to prevent the channels from getting blocked.' Then he continued menacingly: 'I hold you responsible for seeing to it that every twelve minutes the loads are stoked, and don't forget to switch on the fans. Today it's working flat out, understood?'

'Yes, *Herr Oberscharführer*,' cried the two *Kapos*.

'And another thing,' Voss snapped, 'when you've finished, clean up everything, you know, hosing down, chlorinating, and all that sort of thing. And to finish up, lime-wash the walls! Everything clear? By 8 tomorrow morning everything's got to be ship-shape! Off you go!'

About 500 dead bodies were still lying in heaps in the changing room. They must now be sorted according to their combustibility: for the corpses of the well-nourished were to help burn the emaciated. Under the direction of the *Kapos*, the bearers began sorting the dead into four stacks. The largest consisted mainly of strong men, the next in size of women, then came children, and lastly a stack of dead *Mussulmans*, emaciated and nothing but skin and bones. This technique was called 'express work', a designation thought up by the *Kommandoführers* and originating from experiments carried out in crematorium 5 in the autumn of 1943. The purpose of these experiments was to find a way of saving coke. On a few occasions groups of SS men and civilians visited the crematorium to watch the experiments. From conversations between Voss and Gorges we gathered that the civilians were technicians employed by the firm of Topf and Sons of Erfurt who had manufactured and installed the cremation ovens.

In the course of these experiments corpses were selected according to different criteria and then cremated. Thus the corpses of two *Mussulmans* were cremated together with those of two children or the bodies of two well-nourished men together with that of an emaciated woman, each load consisting of three, or sometimes, four bodies. Members of these groups were especially interested in the amount of coke required to burn corpses of any particular category, and in the time it took to cremate them. During these macabre experiments different kinds of coke were used and the results carefully recorded.

Afterwards, all corpses were divided into the above-mentioned four categories, the criterion being the amount of coke required to reduce them to ashes. Thus it was decreed that the most economical and fuel-saving procedure would be to burn the bodies of a well-nourished man and an emaciated woman, or vice versa, together with that of a child, because, as the experiments had established, in this combination, once they had caught fire, the dead would continue to burn without any further coke being required.

As the number of people being gassed grew apace, the four crematoria in Birkenau, even though they were working round the clock with two shifts, could no longer cope with their workload. According to the makers' instructions the ovens required cooling down at regular intervals, repairs needed to be done and the channels leading to the chimneys to be cleaned out. These unavoidable interruptions resulted in the 'quota' of no more than three corpses to each oven load being kept to only very rarely.

The decision as to whether it was to be 'express' or 'normal' work was taken by the *Kommandoführers*. If outsiders or perhaps even the *Lagerkommandant* arrived at the crematorium for an inspection we switched over to normal work immediately. On such occasions Voss and his *Kommandoführers* would put on a grand performance. They pretended to pay meticulous attention to the strict observing of instructions, bustling about in a show of efficiency, ordering us around, hustling us along and generally creating the impression that the smooth running of the crematorium was their sole purpose in life. And if a stoker dared to push his iron fork against the fire-brick lining, if the fans were not switched off in time, or if anything else unforeseen occurred there would be much shouting on the part of the SS. 'Can't you watch what you're doing, you bloody Jewish bastard,' they would yell. 'Watch it, or you'll end up inside the oven too!' Once the visitors had gone 'express work' continued at the usual pace, significantly raising the output of the ovens.

In crematorium 5 the most floor space was taken up by the changing room, about 300 square metres. With its exposed rafters it looked just like a spacious barn. The changing room was on the same level as the two gas chambers and the cremation room. As in the other crematoria its scanty furnishings consisted of wooden benches, numbered clothes-hooks and signboards along the walls. However, there was in crematoria 4 and 5 one signboard whose inscription was actually correct. It was the one which referred to return 'after the bath'. For in these two crematoria the changing rooms served also as mortuaries: after each gassing the corpses had to be dragged back there from the gas chamber. Nowhere were the omnipresence and inexorability of death more obvious than in this place. Because of our constant handling of the dead we seemed to forget they were corpses. We would talk to them as if they were still alive, and even though there was no reply it appeared to worry no one, for we supplied our own answers.

Our working day began early in the morning when we lined up in the fenced barrack yard, ready to march off to the death factories. There the next twelve hours were completely taken up with hard labour. The generators had to be declinkered; the dead dragged to the ovens for cremation, having first had their gold teeth wrenched out and the women their hair cut off; coke had to be brought in; ashes had to be raked out, and finally the crematorium had to be cleaned and disinfected. For our tormentors all this was hard but perfectly normal work; as for us, while we were in the crematorium, we lost all sense of reality. It was not until the late afternoon when we assembled in the yard of the death factory ready to return to camp that life came back to our numbed minds. Birds were singing in the copse near by, fellow prisoners were walking about, the orchestra was playing a rousing march as we entered the camp, sufficient proof that there was a life which went on, even if next morning human bodies in their thousands would once more be turned to dust and ashes.

It was well into the night, and still the carriers were busy dragging corpses from the four heaps into the cremation room. There they were laid on their backs, their mouths prised open and gold teeth, caps and bridges removed. Teeth were never pulled but wrenched out: because of the rush the men who had to prepare the corpses for 'express' processing – all of whom were qualified dentists and oral surgeons – had no choice. By falsely telling them that they were urgently needed for work in dental out-patient clinics the SS had lured them into this hell. And now they were, like the rest of us, corpses waiting their turn.

When *Oberscharführer* Voss returned to the mortuary after a good sleep he found only a few dead bodies left. The 'express' cremation had been a success and Voss was pleased with himself at the thought of a difficult job well done. Presently the strains of marching music drifted across, a sign that soon the day-shift would be on its way to relieve us. 'And high time, too!' I thought. Having read with my own eyes what was to happen to the inmates of the Family Camp, every minute seemed like an eternity to me. I was keenly aware that something must be done to save these people. It was fortunate that three friends of mine, all of them experienced members of the Resistance, were on night-shift with me. While Voss was sleeping off the party, I went to them in the mortuary. When I had reported all I had learnt earlier, we considered how best to help the people in the Family Camp: it was clear to all of us that we must warn them and call upon them to fight, but how this was to be done no one knew. The great haste with which, this night, the extermination of the Jews in the Family Camp was being prepared, alarmed us all. We were in no doubt that the gassing of these people was to take place the following night. Thus we were faced with the urgent question of how, in the brief time left to us, we might contact the Family Camp. And even if we could successfully do this, it seemed doubtful whether the people would actually believe us when we told them what was in store for them. Would they understand that they had nothing to lose, nothing but their lives which were forfeited anyhow? Would they be ready to defend them to their last breath? We did not know the answers to these questions but we thought we must at all costs warn the people and try to convince them that their one chance of survival lay in offering resistance.

Relief came at last. We managed hastily to inform a few members of the day-shift of the night's events. At the same time we asked them to pass on the information to prisoners working in crematoria 2 and 3. Contacting them was no problem since in crematorium 2 were the stores for the entire cremation plant. It was there we collected cleaning and disinfecting materials, as well as building materials like cement, fire-clay, and bricks. All it needed to get there was a pretext.

In the course of the morning I met Kaminski and a few others as they were fetching soup from the camp kitchen. Once more I reported on the contents of the message from the political department. Kaminski was the first to grasp the nub of the matter, saying that the situation was even more serious than appeared to be the case at first glance since, for the last two hours, the fires in crematoria 2 and 3 were being kept going. Everything indicated that the Jews living in the Family Camp were to be gassed during the coming night.

After a brief pause for thought Kaminski abruptly turned to me and decided: 'Go at once and contact your countrymen in the repair shop. They must go to the Family Camp as quickly as possible and warn the people there, preparing them for the worst and explaining that they have only one chance: they must resist and defend themselves. To begin with, they must set their barracks on fire; then they must try to break through the barbed wire into the rest of the camp. And then, together with the rest of their fellow prisoners, they must burn all the wooden barracks to the ground. They must be persuaded that they may rely on us and that we shall all join in. On our part we shall attempt to destroy the crematorium buildings and finish off our tormentors. With a bit of luck we'll manage to escape into the mountains.'

Kaminski's firm and determined words filled me with courage and confidence. At first glance his plan seemed promising. Surely there could be no better allies for a revolt, and none more ready to fight, than people whose extermination was already decided. These Jews had lived here for almost six months, and the mass murders committed daily had not remained hidden from them. They would be ready to rise in revolt because they had no choice.

In a state of great agitation I hurried to the repair shop during the lunch-break. There I met three fellow prisoners with whom I had long been on friendly terms. One of them, Erich Schoen, had his wife and son living in the Family Camp. When I told them of the imminent liquidation of the Family Camp and also of Kaminski's plan, they were ready to go to the Family Camp at once. I asked them not to tell anyone that it was I who had brought them this bad news. It was not difficult for the repair-shop workers to get inside the Family Camp for they were responsible for maintenance. Since often they had to carry out urgent repairs they had passes for every part of the camp.

While they were making their way to the Family Camp, I went to Block 9 where Alfred Wetzler, another friend of mine, was block clerk. He and I had been at school together: of the 634 men deported to Auschwitz from Sered on 13 April 1942 he and I were, in this February of 1944, among the last seven survivors. I told Alfred the dreadful news, at the same time explaining our plans to him. He thought Kaminski's decision correct in the circumstances, but doubted whether we would succeed in coming to an understanding with the inmates of the Family Camp in so short a time. His misgivings made me feel uneasy, for I knew him as a shrewd and fearless man, well able to distinguish between reality and wishful thinking. At that time he and another prisoner had already made up their minds to escape and were busy with their preparations. Now here was I with the news of plans for a revolt which might well cut across their own plans to escape.

My three friends from the repair-shop returned, alarmed and disappointed. The people in the Family Camp did not want to know about the peril in which they found themselves. Since their arrival in Birkenau they had enjoyed so many privileges that the idea that they might be gassed seemed absurd. Why, they asked, had they been taken here with their families and left unmolested all this time if it had been intended to kill them? The Nazis could have killed them in Theresienstadt. Why had they been allowed to build their own camp? Surely not in order to gas them now that they had finished building it? Many regarded the bad news the repair workers had delivered as an unreliable rumour, while others looked upon it as some kind of deliberate attempt to cause panic, with the aim of getting them involved in a hazardous attempt to escape.

Late in the afternoon the day-shift returned to camp from the crematoria. Much to our surprise the night-shift did not leave for work which meant that the fire in the ovens was no longer kept going. I noticed this fact with some relief. Perhaps the date for the murder campaign was postponed so that there would still be time to convince the threatened inmates of the Family Camp of their danger and persuade them into joint action.

A few days passed without any change in the daily routine of the Family Camp. Thus the credibility of our warnings was eroded, and they were regarded simply as an attempt to involve peaceable people in an irresponsible and perilous adventure at all costs.

But the calm did not last. I learned from the repairmen that a Slovak woman prisoner who acted as secretary to *SS-Oberaufseherin** Mandel had overheard an SS man in a telephone conversation with Berlin during which details of the liquidation of the Family Camp were discussed. The news quickly spread throughout the camp. Once more we tried to convince the threatened people of their danger. In vain! Even the camp Resistance stepped in and appealed to the people in the Family Camp to defend themselves against being gassed. None of us succeeded in moving them an inch. The fact was that they were simply not prepared for a struggle. Besides, they lacked men with energy, determination and authority sufficiently strong-willed to assume the leadership. There was Fredi Hirsch, a young German Jew, who enjoyed the respect and esteem of everyone in the Family Camp because he devoted himself in an exemplary and selfless manner to the education of children and young people. But he lacked not only the necessary toughness and determination but also the experience of coping with critical situations to be a leader. And who else was there to stand up for Czech Jews when they were themselves not determined to venture their uttermost? What was it that kept these people from committing themselves to resistance?

In the period between the two world wars the Jews of Bohemia and Moravia lived in liberal, democratic and economically flourishing society. Without constraint they adapted themselves to prevailing conditions, taking an active part in the social and cultural life of the country. Thus they succeeded in gaining the confidence, liking and friendship of most of their fellow citizens. However, among themselves they were split into numerous groups and parties. In addition they had no co-ordinating central authority. There were among them members of the upper and lower middle classes, craftsmen and labourers, members of the political Left, liberals, intellectuals without political or ideological commitment, and Zionists. The majority were tolerant, ready to compromise, and with democratic leanings.

When on 15 March 1939 the Nazis invaded Bohemia and Moravia, the 118,000 Jews living there viewed the event with misgivings; but it was altogether beyond anybody's wildest imagination to envisage in this twentieth century the systematic extermination of an entire ethnic group. It was only a few days after the occupation before what was known as racial legislation was implemented. To begin with all Jews were removed from the Civil Service. Their factories and business firms were 'Aryanized'. Jewish doctors were forbidden to treat panel patients or, for that matter, to work in any branch of the national health organization. Gradually the Jews were debarred from the political, economic, cultural and social life of the country until they had been completely excluded. Their rights were more and more curtailed. They were forced to declare their assets and to surrender their radio sets, musical instruments, skiing equipment and furs. Their identity cards were marked with a large J. From the age of seven they had to wear the yellow Star of David on their clothing. They were allowed out of their homes only until 8 p.m. They were not allowed to move house, nor were they any longer permitted to leave their address for any purpose whatever without a permit. Marriage with non-Jews was forbidden, as were visits to parks and public gardens, swimming baths, cinemas, theatres and sports grounds. They were not allowed to attend secondary schools or universities. Shopping times for Jews were restricted; they were not allowed to have their hair cut by non-Jewish barbers, nor were they permitted to send their washing to the laundry. On trams there were a very few standing places at the rear reserved for Jews. Jews were much harder hit by food rationing than the rest of the Czech population. Thus they were not allowed to store potatoes or to buy garlic. They were no longer allowed to keep domestic animals so that they were forced to part from their dogs, cats and birds. Having been deserted by almost all their non-Jewish friends, mostly from fear of reprisals, they were entirely left to their own devices without a single possibility of influencing the course of their own fate in any way. The majority put off emigration for as long as possible, for despite their tribulations Czechoslovakia was their homeland and they were loath to leave it. There would be time enough, many thought at first, to flee the country. Their hopes and actions were all geared towards one end: to gain time and to survive the war, however arduous the conditions. These expectations were sustained by constant and new rumours, from Hitler's serious illnesses to imminent diplomatic intervention on the part of Stalin and Roosevelt to protect Czech Jews, and these rumours prevented many from emigrating.

Thus, day by day, their situation grew more difficult and

hopeless. A few isolated international protests failed to make any impact. There was no one ready to take effectual steps on their behalf. But even the steadily increasing stream of harassments, humiliations and bullyings failed to give to the stricken Jews an inkling of the far worse troubles which were to befall them. After the whole world had turned its back on them they were robbed of almost all their personal belongings and, from November 1941, transported to the model ghetto of Theresienstadt. The comparatively tolerable conditions there were meant to lead the outside world to believe that the Nazis, willing to show a minimum of humaneness even to the Jews, were at least respecting their lives. The existence of the ghetto was therefore meant to counteract those rumours that there was a mass extermination of Jews. The truth was that the ghetto of Theresienstadt was a collecting point and transit stage for Jews on their way to the extermination camps in the East.

It was from this ghetto that the majority of people had come who lived in the Family Camp and whose death by gassing had now been decreed. Concern for their children and also for their old and sick further stifled their not very strong will to defend themselves. The thought that if they resisted they might have to witness the slaughter of their wives and children made them recoil. If death was inevitable, then they would rather die together in the gas chamber.

To be perfectly honest, our own idea of organizing an uprising throughout the camp with the help of the Resistance was probably no more than wishful thinking. To gain the co-operation of the Resistance at that very moment was not as easy as it might seem at first sight: the majority of prisoners in the Resistance movement had gone through a great deal of suffering; the approach of the Red Army led them to hope, with good reason, that they had a genuine chance of survival, a chance which was increasing daily. Were they then to risk their lives in a desperate and perilous struggle for a few thousand Czech Jews and 200 prisoners of the *Sonderkommando*? As everybody hesitated and held back, the inevitable and tragic end for the Family Camp came a few days later. The SS had asked inmates to write to relatives or friends post-dating their letters; the ostensible reason for this was that mail had first to be sent to Berlin for censoring.

A few days later *Lagerführer* Schwarzhuber visited the Family Camp and announced that a number of inmates and their families were to be transported to Heydebreck to work there. Soon afterwards about 3,700 Czech Jews who had arrived from Theresienstadt in September 1943 were transferred to quarantine camp B2. Prior to their transfer they had to take a bath and be disinfected in the sauna, this being the procedure for all prisoners who were either to be transferred or released. This was bound to reinforce most people in their belief that they would really be taken to Heydebreck.

Together with some hundred fellow prisoners I went on duty in the two death factories during the late afternoon of 8 March 1944. After dark heavy trucks began to rumble into the yard of crematorium 2. SS men undid the tarpaulins and lowered the tailboards. Then they viciously clubbed the people with their truncheons as they were climbing and jumping down. A further group of SS guards made them run the gauntlet into the underground changing room; the whole gruesome scene was illuminated by floodlights. Today the SS showed no consideration for the old, the sick or for children, beating and clubbing everybody without mercy.

Burst at last like a soap bubble was the persistent rumour that the Family Camp stood under the protection of the International Red Cross. Today the SS – who in the past might well have helped to keep that rumour alive – dispensed with camouflage and any of their usual cover-up activities. For, as they entered the crematorium yard, these people who had lived in Birkenau for six months, who had seen the crematorium chimneys belching smoke and fumes day after day after day, left behind any illusions they might still have harboured. The SS was fully aware of this: so instead of the customary act of deception they treated their victims on their last journey with a brutality that beggared description.

It was not long before the first 600 or so people were inside the crematorium changing room. There they had to wait for their fellow victims to arrive. The SS men had them where they wanted them and no longer paid any attention to them.

Together with about thirty prisoners I was in the underground passage which linked the changing room to the gas chamber. After the gassing it would be our job to load the garments left behind on a truck in the yard. Strictly speaking, as a stoker I had no business here at all, but ties of a common past, a common language, religion and culture drew me near to these people in their last hour. The scene through the half-open door of the changing room was heart-rending. Groups of desperate people were crowding round the fake signboards. When they were still living in the Family Camp they had heard many a tale about these strange rooms; but then, despite much obvious proof, they did not wish to know about them. Now they were here themselves and realized, too late, that all they had heard was indeed true. They knew that the signboards were fake, and in their frightened eyes I could read fear and despair. Young mothers were clasping their little ones to their breast, while older boys and girls clung weeping to their parents' legs.

On the stairs next to the exit stood SS guards with a pack of Alsatians which were barking furiously and pulling at their leads, excited, no doubt, by the smell of blood. People's blood-stained and battered heads and faces proved that there was scarcely anyone who had been able to dodge the truncheon blows in the yard. Their faces were ashen with fear and grief. Now, near their end and conscious of it, there were many who saw through the web of lies and contradictions with which they had allowed themselves to be deluded. Why had they and their families been allowed to live unmolested in Birkenau for six months? Why only a few days ago had *Lagerführer* Schwarzhuber promised them on his word of honour as an SS leader that they and their families would be going to Heydebreck? Why had the sick been promised that they would follow onto Heydebreck as soon as they were well again? Why had a special list with the names of prisoners employed by the camp administration been drawn up, and why had they been given the assurance that in Heydebreck they would be doing the same jobs? Why, only a few days ago, had they been invited to write letters to their relatives? Why had they been transferred to the quarantine camp, and why had they been given food rations for their supposed journey to Heydebreck? Why, why, why? Surely none of this had been necessary, for they were not prepared for resistance or for defending their lives. They had no arms, and how else could they have defended themselves? All these questions for which no answers could be found, filled the people with bitterness. Hope and illusions had vanished; what was left was disappointment, despair and anger.

They began to bid each other farewell. Husbands embraced their wives and children. Everybody was in tears. Mothers turned to their children and caressed them tenderly. The little ones sensed that something frightening was about to happen. They wept with their mothers and held on to them. But gradually the people's sorrow changed to restlessness and agitation. When several SS leaders, among them *Lagerführer* Schwarzhuber and Dr Mengele, appeared in the doorway of the changing room, those standing near flew into a rage: suffering and sorrow gave way to unrestrained hatred for those men who had made false promises and given their word of honour that they would be taken to work at Heydebreck.

This time the cynicism of the executioners knew no bounds. Today they gave up any tricks of deception and disguise. Self-confidently they stood in front of the changing room and looked without pity at the crowd of people. One could tell that they were satisfied with the way the extermination had gone up to now.

Now a few people began to shout slogans, their cries growing louder as they were joined by their fellows. 'We want to live!' they cried, and 'We want to work!' Their angry voices echoed across the underground room. It was their stubborn will to live which made them regard this ante-room of death as a place from which they might still escape. When they saw that their appeals met with no response from the SS leaders, some of the men rushed towards the door. No doubt they wanted to confront Schwarzhuber and remind him of his 'word of honour'. But their plan was foiled. Once they reached the door they were instantly shot by armed SS guards, some fifty of whom were in the crematorium that day. There was also a large number of *SS-Unterführer*s, among them Boger, Buntrock, Baretzki, Hustek, Steinberg, Kurschuss, Schulz and Gorges. After the shootings, the SS men once more flung themselves upon the wretched crowd in the changing room; beating them about the head with their truncheons and using their Alsatians they drove them into the back of the room. Then they erected machine-guns in front of them.

I feared that they were all going to be shot and turned away from the half-open door because I could not bear to watch the massacre. But when, against all expectations, no shots were fired, I turned back again. The people, crowded together on one side of the room, were shaking with terror. Almost all of them were now sobbing: their weeping sounded like a heart-breaking dirge. Most of them were badly hurt from truncheon blows as well as from the sharp teeth of the dogs.

The SS must have realized that they could not afford to let the second lot of victims into the changing room where their fellow victims no longer bore any resemblance to God's image. Therefore *Oberscharführer* Voss stepped in front of the crowd in an endeavour to establish contact with them. Raising his hands pleadingly he turned to the people to give them to understand that they should be quiet. Once there was silence, he began to speak: 'Now, what is the meaning of all this, you Jews? Your hour has come. There is nothing in the world which can reverse your fate. It is entirely up to you. If you are sensible, you can spare yourselves and your children a great deal of distress. A great deal,' he re-emphasized. The words reiterated by Voss had a strange effect on the crowd who thought that if they could spare themselves and their children a great deal of distress it must mean that there was still some hope. But before they had time to follow up this thought, Voss continued: 'Everything will be much easier if you get undressed quickly and then move on into the next room. Or do you want to make your children's last moments needlessly distressing?'

At last they had been told straight to their faces what awaited them. There was no misunderstanding Voss's words now. Their voices grew subdued and tense, their movements forced, their eyes stared as though they had been hypnotized. The atmosphere in the room was one of immense gravity. Most of the people now began to undress, but some were still hesitating. As soon as the executioners perceived this they pushed and shoved the crowd into the gas chamber, irrespective of whether or not they had taken off their clothes. Anybody offering resistance was mercilessly beaten to a pulp. Husbands, helpless themselves, crowded round their wives and children to protect them from blows and also from the savage teeth of the dogs. There was chaos as in the narrow space people pushed and shoved each other, SS men shouted and used their truncheons, and dogs barked and snapped ferociously.

Suddenly a voice began to sing. Others joined in, and the sound swelled into a mighty choir. They sang first the Czechoslovak national anthem and then the Hebrew song 'Hatikvah'. And all this time the SS men never stopped their brutal beatings. It was as if they regarded the singing as a last kind of protest which they were determined to stifle if they could. To be allowed to die together was the only comfort left to these people. Singing their national anthem they were saying a last farewell to their brief but flourishing past, a past which had enabled them to live for twenty years in a democratic state, a respected minority enjoying equal rights. And when they sang 'Hatikvah', now the national anthem of the state of Israel, they were glancing into the future, but it was a future which they would not be allowed to see.

To me the bearing of my countrymen seemed an exemplary gesture of national honour and national pride which stirred my soul. I proudly identified with them. After all that I had gone through I felt that to go on clinging to my hopeless existence was totally senseless. I knew that next spring would not fulfil my expectations either. After all, had we not been told by the Resistance only a few days ago that an escape was not feasible as long as the front was still a long way off?

Now, when I watched my fellow countrymen walk into the gas chamber, brave, proud and determined, I asked myself what sort of life it would be for me in the unlikely event of my getting out of the camp alive. What would await me if I returned to my native town? It was not so much a matter of material possessions, they were replaceable. But who could replace my parents, my brother, or the rest of my family, of whom I was the sole survivor? And what of friends, teachers, and the many members of our Jewish community? For was it not they who reminded me of my childhood and youth? Without them would it not all be soulless and dead, that familiar outline of my home town with its pretty river, its much loved landscape and its honest and upright citizens? And what would happen if I ran across the Hlinka guardsmen and Jew tormentors, or the FS men*, leeches all of them who had sucked their Jewish fellow citizens dry before their deportation and stolen their worldly belongings? Coming face to face with them would take me back to the darkest past. It would simply not be possible to pick up the threads of my former happy and carefree life. In our house, once the centre of my existence, there would be strangers. In the Jewish school where I knew every nook and cranny there would be silence. And what would have become of the synagogue where my grandfather would take me on the sabbath? No doubt it had been ransacked and turned into a gymnasium or some such secular building. Strange to say, at that moment I felt quite free from that tormenting fear of death which had often almost overwhelmed me before. I had never yet contemplated the possibility of taking my own life, but now I was determined to share the fate of my countrymen.

In the great confusion near the door I managed to mingle with the pushing and shoving crowd of people who were being driven into the gas chamber. Quickly I ran to the back and stood behind one of the concrete pillars. I thought that here I would remain undiscovered until the gas chamber was full, when it would be locked. Until then I must try to remain unnoticed. I was overcome by a feeling of indifference: everything had become meaningless. Even the thought of a painful death from Zyclon B gas, whose effect I of all people knew only too well, no long filled me with fear and horror. I faced my fate with composure.

Inside the gas chamber the singing had stopped. Now there was only weeping and sobbing. People, their faces smashed and bleeding, were still streaming through the door, driven by blows and goaded by vicious dogs. Desperate children who had become separated from their parents in the scramble were rushing around calling for them. All at once, a small boy was standing before me. He looked at me curiously; perhaps he had noticed me there at the back standing all by myself. Then, his little face puckered with worry, he asked timidly: 'Do you know where my mummy and my daddy are hiding?' I tried to comfort him, explaining that his parents were sure to be among all those people milling round in the front part of the room. 'You run along there,' I told him, 'and they'll be waiting for you, you'll see.'

The child scampered off, and as I looked up I found that a group of some fifteen people had gathered round me. Some of them were naked, others still wore their clothes. They looked at me puzzled and to my surprise one of them addressed me by my first name. When I looked more closely I recognized him as the Family Camp's clerk, while next to him stood the deputy block senior, both of whom I had met once when I had sneaked into the Family Camp with the repair workers' team. My plan to die anonymously was frustrated. The people who had recognized me insisted on my explaining to them why I had decided to die with them. I implored them not to speak to anybody about my decision; for I knew that it would probably take some time before the gas chamber was sealed off. And until then I wanted to remain undiscovered. During our conversation they told me that young Fredi Hirsch who had so devotedly cared for the young people in the Family Camp had committed suicide.

Time seemed to stand still. The minutes dragged on, and there was no end, no release from torment, in sight. Outside, at the doors to the gas chamber, stood *Unterführer*s Voss, Gorges and

Kurschuss, and behind them armed SS guards with their dogs which barked incessantly, all of them obviously waiting for the next truck load of people to arrive. Through the open door I saw Schwarzhuber and Dr Mangele stretching to look curiously over the guards' shoulders into the gas chamber. When they were recognized renewed shouts and curses sounded in the gas chamber. 'You have cheated us! But your Hitler will lose the war! Then will come the hour of revenge. Then you will have to pay for everything, murderers!' Accusations and angry exclamations like these were hurled passionately at the door. The executioners were unmoved; they remained mute. My one regret was that, at this fateful hour, I did not have one of our three hand-grenades with me. But I made my decision to die on the spur of the moment; there had been neither time nor opportunity for special preparations.

The atmosphere in the dimly lit gas chamber was tense and depressing. Death had come menacingly close. It was only minutes away. No memory, no trace of any of us would remain. Once more people embraced. Parents were hugging their children so violently that it almost broke my heart. Suddenly a few girls, naked and in the full bloom of youth, came up to me. They stood in front of me without a word, gazing at me deep in thought and shaking their heads uncomprehendingly. At last one of them plucked up courage and spoke to me: 'We understand that you have chosen to die with us of your own free will, and we have come to tell you that we think your decision pointless: for it helps no one.' She went on: '*We* must die, but you still have a chance to save your life. You have to return to the camp and tell everybody about our last hours,' she commanded. 'You have to explain to them that they must free themselves from any illusions. They ought to fight, that's better than dying here helplessly. It'll be easier for them, since they have no children. As for you, perhaps you'll survive this terrible tragedy and then you must tell everybody what happened to you. One more thing,' she went on, 'you can do me one last favour: this gold chain round my neck: when I'm dead, take it off and give it to my boyfriend Sasha. He works in the bakery. Remember me to him. Say "love from Yana". When it's all over, you'll find me here.' She pointed at a place next to the concrete pillar where I was standing. Those were her last words.

I was surprised and strangely moved by her cool and calm

detachment in the face of death, and also by her sweetness. Before I could make an answer to her spirited speech, the girls took hold of me and dragged me protesting to the door of the gas chamber. There they gave me a last push which made me land bang in the middle of the group of SS men. Kurschuss was the first to recognize me and at once set about me with his truncheon. I fell to the floor, stood up and was knocked down by a blow from his fist. As I stood on my feet for the third or fourth time, Kurschuss yelled at me: 'You bloody shit, get it into your stupid head: *we* decide how long you stay alive and when you die, and not you. Now piss off, to the ovens!' Then he socked me viciously in the face so that I reeled against the lift door.

I took the lift upstairs and went into the cremation room. There my legs gave way under me, my head was spinning, and I knew I was going to faint. When I came to, I was lying in the coke store. Some of my fellow prisoners helped me up and took me to the door for a breath of fresh air. I stood there wiping the cold sweat from my forehead, my heart beating furiously with fearful foreboding. I asked for a cigarette and a light and tried to pretend that I had not a care in the world, while all the time my nerves were strung to breaking point. And then Kaminski arrived. He tried to make me understand that my nerves had got the better of me and that anything like that, even though he had full understanding for it, must not happen again. 'You would not want to please our tormentors,' he said, 'by dying without putting up a fight, particularly not now when we need you more than ever. You are still young: it is vital that you should see everything, experience everything, go through everything and consciously record everything in your mind. Maybe you are one of those who one day will be free.' He had spoken in firm and commanding tones, at the same time slapping me encouragingly on the shoulder. 'Now off you go, and get hold of a fork or something, so that they don't catch you skiving!' With these words he left me.

Following his advice I grabbed one of the iron forks, just in case an SS guard might suddenly turn up, when I would pretend to be busy loading coke onto a wheelbarrow. Kaminski's remarks had comforted and encouraged me. Once again I was determined to go on fighting for my life. Perhaps there would be a miracle, perhaps one day I would be free.

I could hear trucks driving into the yard: the second convoy had arrived. Again SS men were shouting, again dogs were barking.

Try though I might not to think of what was at that moment happening in the gas chamber, my thoughts kept returning there. In my mind's eye I again saw Yana with her long black hair. Her regular features, her slim body, her passionate eyes flashing with righteous indignation; her instinctively well-chosen words, had made a deep impression on me. I realized that I had no idea who she was. Perhaps Sasha, her lover, who worked in the breadstore would tell me. For a brief moment I thought of him. How would he take it when he heard about the death of his beloved Yana? Then my thoughts wandered to some of my companions in the camp who were preparing their escape and for whom I had promised to obtain pieces of evidence, such as the labels on the tins containing Zyclon B gas. By now I had come back to reality. I hoped that perhaps I might be of use to the Resistance, although I was still very young and without much experience of life. Thus, within a few hours, I had come to the conviction that each minute, each hour and each day I could interpose between the day of my death was a gift from heaven.

The ambulance, marked on the back and on both sides with the emblem of the Red Cross, entered the crematorium yard, but today it stopped behind the building so as to remain unnoticed. On unsuspecting prisoners newly arrived at the crematorium the presence of the ambulance usually had a reassuring effect. But for people who had lived in the camp for some time, the opposite would probably have been the case. For they would have heard rumours concerning the reason why the ambulance was parked outside the crematorium. The vehicle had stopped alongside the lawn behind the crematorium where the concrete shafts projected, through which the pea-sized grains of Zyclon B gas were introduced. Near by the two 'disinfecting operators' were ready and waiting for their orders to pour in the gas crystals. But the time had clearly not yet come; for the two were chatting leisurely and lighting cigarettes. Although by now there were more than 1,000 people in the gas chamber, more were obviously expected. In fact, before long a third convoy of trucks moved into the yard. Once more the people were driven into the changing room with the utmost brutality.

After a while I heard the sound of piercing screams, banging against the door and also moaning and wailing. People began to cough. Their coughing grew worse from minute to minute, a sign that the gas had started to act. Then the clamour began to subside and to change to a many-voiced dull rattle, drowned now and then by coughing. The deadly gas had penetrated into the lungs of the people where it quickly caused paralysis of the respiratory centre.

It seemed to me that today death came more swiftly than usual. Barely ten minutes had passed since the introduction of the gas crystals when there was quiet in the gas chamber. Possibly the reason was that the concrete floor was quite dry or perhaps today the 'disinfecting operators' had thrown in a few more tinfuls of Zyclon B than usual. It was a fact established by experience that whenever Zyclon B crystals came into contact with water or were exposed to humidity the gas was prevented from taking full effect.

Even before the door of the gas chamber was due to be opened, the SS guards with their dogs, the *Unterführers* as well as several other SS men went across to crematorium 3. After they had left, the 'disinfecting operators' car with its Red Cross camouflage followed across to the crematorium yard. This meant that the gassings were to be continued there.

On the order of an SS man I had taken the lift down again in the company of a few other prisoners. As we stepped out of the lift, *Lagerführer* Schwarzhuber and Dr Mengele were standing outside the door to the gas chamber. The doctor was just switching on the light. Then he bent forward and peered through a peep-hole in the door to ascertain whether there were still any signs of life inside. After a while he ordered the *Kommandoführer* to switch on the fans which were to disperse the gas. When they had run for a few minutes the door to the gas chamber which was secured with a few horizontal bolts was opened.

Even before the bottom bar had been unbolted both wings of the double doors were bulging to the outside under the weight of the bodies. As the doors opened, the top layer of corpses tumbled out like the contents of an overloaded truck when the tail-board is let down. They were the strongest who, in their mortal terror, had instinctively fought their way to the door, the one and only way out, had there been even the remotest possibility of getting out. It was the same every time the gas chamber was used. Moreover, the bodies were not evenly distributed throughout the chamber; most of them lay in heaps, the largest of which was always by the door. The spot where the gas came in was practically empty: no doubt the people had moved away from these places because the gas smelled of burning metaldehyde and had a sickly-sweet taste.

After a short time it produced an excruciating irritation of the throat and intense pressure in the head, before it took its lethal effect.

We had orders that immediately after the opening of the gas chamber we were to take away first the corpses that had tumbled out, followed by those lying behind the door, so as to clear a path. This was done by putting the loop of a leather strap round the wrist of a corpse and then dragging the body to the lift by the strap and thence conveying it upstairs to the crematorium. When some room had been made behind the door, the corpses were hosed down. This served to neutralize any gas crystals still lying about, but mainly it was intended to clean the dead bodies. For almost all of them were wet with sweat and urine, filthy with blood and excrement, while the legs of many women were streaked with menstrual blood.

As soon as Zyclon B crystals came into contact with air the deadly gas began to develop, spreading first at floor level and then rising to the ceiling. It was for this reason that the bottom layer of corpses always consisted of children as well as the old and the weak, while the tallest and strongest lay on top, with middle-aged men and women in between. No doubt the ones on top had climbed up there over the bodies already lying on the floor because they still had the strength to do so and perhaps also because they had realized that the deadly gas was spreading from the bottom upwards. The people in their heaps were intertwined some lying in each other's arms, others holding each other's hands; groups of them were leaning against the walls, pressed against each other like columns of basalt.

The carriers had great difficulty in prising the corpses apart, even though they were still warm and not yet rigid. Many had their mouths wide open, on their lips traces of whitish dried-up spittle. Many had turned blue, and many faces were disfigured almost beyond recognition from blows. No doubt the subterranean labyrinth into which the gas chamber had turned when the lights went out, had led the people in their panic to rush all over the place, bump against each other, fall on top of each other and trample one another, thus causing this confusion of tangled-up corpses. Among them lay the bodies of pregnant women, some of whom had expressed the head of their baby just before they died.

During the removal of corpses from the gas chamber bearers

117

had to wear gas-masks because the fans were unable to disperse the gas completely. In particular there were remnants of the lethal gas in between the dead bodies, and this was released during cleaning out operations. It was terrible but also strenuous work to disentangle the corpses and then to drag them away. It quickly made me sweat so that the glasses of my gas-mask steamed up. Every few minutes I had to stop to catch my breath. When the bearers had begun to remove the corpses from the back of the gas chamber, I went to the pillar near which the girls had talked to me. There I found the girl Yana who had asked me to take off her necklace and give it to her lover as a last keepsake. She lay where she had said she would. I took off the necklace, pocketed it and left the room.

As soon as I returned to the camp I went to the breadstore. On my way there I learned that one of the block seniors, a *Reichsdeutscher* named Roehrig who wore the political prisoners' red triangle, had been transferred to the penal company, having had his head shaved first. Last night, before the inmates of the Family Camp were driven into trucks to take them from the quarantine camp to the crematorium, the SS had armed *Kapo*s and block seniors with truncheons, ordering them to take part in the brutal round-up. This particular block senior had refused to join in, telling the SS men that he for one was no executioner.

I found Sasha in the breadstore. He came from Odessa and had been a non-commissioned officer in the Red Army when he was taken prisoner of war. In 1941 – together with about 13,000 Soviet prisoners of war of whom, by January 1945, less than 100 were still alive – he was taken to Auschwitz. Sasha used to smile at me whenever we met, but today his face was serious. Like most prisoners he had heard that the Family Camp was to be liquidated. When I handed him the gold chain and delivered his sweetheart's farewell greetings, the tears ran down his bronzed, scarred face. Overcome by pain and sorrow he could not utter a word. He bowed his head and swallowed hard in an attempt to get the better of his feelings. After a few long minutes of silence his pent-up anguish burst out. '*Moya dorogaya* Yana' (my dear Yana), he cried, sobbing and burying his face in his hands. Afterwards he told me that he had seen Yana for the last time a few weeks ago. They had discussed what they would do if and when they would ever get out of Birkenau. Yana, he said, had not a single person left in the world. All her relations in Prague where she had been working as a children's nurse were dead. So they had decided to go to his mother in Odessa, and to marry there. When Sasha had finished telling me all this, he muttered, his voice choked with tears: 'Now nothing matters any more.'

After the events of the previous night I no longer had the strength to share Sasha's sorrow nor could I find any words of comfort to say to him. With tears in my eyes I turned and left. As I was walking down the camp road I was startled by the brisk command: 'Sing!' Turning round I saw the penal company marching out. Their song rang out in the spring landscape. The prisoners were singing the song of the nut-brown maiden.

Chapter 5
The Inferno

When on 7 April 1944 after evening roll-call the alarm siren began to wail, Alfred Wetzler and Walter Rosenberg-Vrba had been squatting in their narrow underground hideout for a couple of hours. It was beyond the barbed wire which encircled the camp, but still inside the outer cordon which guarded a wider area during the day. Their fox-hole had been dug in the camp called *Mexico** where, at that time, a large camp for thousands of prisoners was under construction. Once Alfred and Walter had crawled inside their burrow, a few prisoners working on the site and let into the plan, covered it, first with wooden boards and then with a layer of soil. Then they drenched the soil and surrounding area with paraffin and sprinkled it with tobacco in order to prevent the dogs from sniffing the two out, a tip which came from Soviet prisoners of war.

Everybody in the camp knew the meaning of the penetrating wailing of the siren: it was the signal that there had been an attempt to escape. In the camps where Wetzler and Rosenberg-Vrba were quartered their absence had been noticed during evening roll-call and the alarm given immediately.

For the next few days the two would have to face a gruelling ordeal. For three days and three nights they must stay crouched in their dark and narrow hiding-place, for the outer cordon was permitted to be withdrawn only if after three days a search was unsuccessful. However, even that was not always the case. For, if there were a further attempt to escape during this period, the cordon would remain in position for another three full days. Finally, it was uncertain how long the two would be able to endure squatting in their fox-hole without either suffocating or being discovered.

The SS camp authorities had taken stringent measures to prevent prisoners escaping. The centre of the camp which housed the prisoners' quarters was surrounded by two 5-metres high electrified barbed-wire fences. This area was guarded by large numbers of SS men who were armed with machine-guns and mainly manned the watch-towers. They made up what was known as the inner cordon which was withdrawn during the day because then most prisoners were working outside the camp where they were guarded by the outer cordon. This was withdrawn only at night after all prisoners had returned to camp and none reported missing during evening roll-call.

As it was growing dark on 7 April 1944, the search machine swung into action. SS men, *Kapo*s, and those barrack seniors who were considered reliable frantically explored every nook and cranny, turning the prison barracks upside down, snooping about in store-rooms and workshops, in wash-rooms and latrines. In the area outside the barbed-wire fences another feverish hunt was in progress. SS men with Alsatian guard-dogs were looking around in *Mexico* where the hiding-place was, searching for the prisoners on the building sites, among building materials and in trenches. All through the night the furious barking and yapping of the dogs could be heard. Trained to attack they could sniff out any unfamiliar smell and hear any noise.

I was pleased to discover next morning that all their efforts had been in vain. Alfred and Walter would succeed in escaping from this hell on earth, of that I now felt much more confident. If they managed to get through they would be sure to accomplish the assignment they had undertaken. When on the evening of the third day after their escape the outer cordon was withdrawn, I heaved a sigh of relief. I had great expectations from the success of their flight. It was from them that, at long last, the world would learn about the death factories of Auschwitz.

I had handed to Alfred a plan of the crematoria and gas chambers as well as a list of names of the SS men who were on duty there. In addition I had given to both of them notes I had been making for some time of almost all transports gassed in crematoria 4 and 5. I had described to them in full detail the process of extermination so that they would be able to report to the outside world exactly how the victims had their last pitiful belongings taken away from them; how they were tricked into entering the gas chambers; how after the gassings their teeth were wrenched out and the women's hair cut off; how the dead were searched for hidden valuables; how their spectacles, artificial limbs and dentures were collected; and everything else that took place. In the course of many long talks I had described to them both the tragedy which was constantly being enacted behind the crematorium walls.

The most important piece of evidence which I gave them to take on their journey was one of those labels which were stuck on the tins containing Zyclon B poison gas. I tried for a long time to lay my hands on one of these tins. This was not an easy matter, though. After the 'disinfecting operators' had poured the lethal gas crystals into the gas chambers one of them took the empty tins back to their Red Cross ambulance while, as a rule, the other walked over to the changing rooms to see if there was any *organizing* to be done. Although on several occasions I was quite close to the ambulance, I never managed to grab hold of one of the tins. I was despairing as it looked as though I would never be able to. And then I had an idea.

One day after the 'disinfecting operators' had finished their handiwork, I informed *Unterscharführer* Gorges that we needed two new tins in which to collect gold teeth because the old ones had become rather dented. Not suspecting my ulterior motive he sent me to the Red Cross ambulance in the yard where I proceeded to explain to the two SS men that *Unterscharführer* Gorges had ordered me to collect two empty tins. One of them took a couple of tins from the back of the ambulance and handed them to me with the words: 'There you are, and now scram!' The text printed on the labels read something like this: *Zyclon B poison gas. Cyanogen compound. Danger! Poison! Tesch and Stabenov International GMBH. For pest control. To be opened by trained personnel only.* It was difficult to get the labels off without damaging them, and I only managed it partly with one of the tins. Where the paper had been torn and the name and address of the manufacturers become somewhat illegible I made the necessary additions in pencil.

Two days before his escape I handed the label to Alfred Wetzler to enable him to produce it as another piece of evidence of the systematic extermination of Jews. Once he and Walter Rosenberg-Vrba had revealed to the world the whole dreadful truth as they knew it about Auschwitz, surely something would be done to put an end to the mass murder. The rest of the world, so I believed, could not remain silent in the face of what was happening here.

Once again I remembered that courageous and determined girl and her young friends who, a month earlier, had pushed me out of the gas chamber, imploring me to go on living; for one day I might bear witness to the sufferings, atrocities and terrors human beings were made to endure here. Now at last the time had come.

In my mind I imagined Allied bombers reducing to ashes both the crematoria and the gas chambers. After that, all it needed to stop transports of Jews reaching Auschwitz was constant bombing of all railway lines leading here. Once my two friends had breached the wall of silence, these slaughter-houses would close their doors forever.

Several days had passed since the escape of Alfred and Walter. The gallows on which the SS intended to hang them after their capture were still pointing menacingly into the sky. I was sure the SS must be racking their brains to work out how those two had managed to get away. By now I no longer doubted that Alfred and Walter were a long way away from the death factories. Our own Resistance leaders renewed their pressure for a signal to start the uprising; but the Resistance in the main camp still deemed it right to go on waiting.

Thus the weeks passed and the sky over Birkenau continued to grow darker. There were daily indications of impending disasters. Although the Red Army was only a few hundred kilometres away from Auschwitz and drawing nearer every day, there was frantic activity in the area around Birkenau. Day and night many hundreds of prisoners were busy laying railway tracks right up to crematoria 2 and 3. On the road between the building sites B1 and B2 the construction of a loading and unloading ramp complete with a three-track railway system was in progress in order to provide a direct link between the death factories, Auschwitz railway station and the outside world. A large number of prisoners were employed on road works. From early morning to late at night there was the incessant din and clatter of trucks, cement-mixers and other building machinery. New prisoners' quarters in camp B2c and also in *Mexico* were nearing completion, while in camp B2g final preparations to ensure efficient handling were made in the barracks housing the personal effects stores. The work-force known as the *Canada team* was gradually built up to a strength of almost 1,000 prisoners. It was their job to load personal belongings, taken from new arrivals on the ramp, on trucks, deliver them to the stores, sort them, search them for valuables, clean all clothing, and get everything ready for despatch to the Reich. All clothing, underwear, shoes, and any other articles left in the changing rooms were also taken to *Canada*.

In addition to several prisoner teams civilian workers from a factory in Upper Silesia were called in to overhaul the crematoria. Cracks in the brickwork of the ovens were filled with a special fire-clay paste; the cast-iron doors were painted black and the door hinges oiled. New grates were fitted in the generators, while the six chimneys underwent a thorough inspection and repair, as did the electric fans. The walls of the four changing rooms and the eight gas chambers were given a fresh coat of paint.

Quite obviously all these efforts were intended to put the places of extermination into peak condition to guarantee smooth and continuous operation. What mystified us not a little, however, was the beautification of crematorium 5, where everything in sight was whitewashed. What was the point of wasting all this white paint when on the first day after operations had started again the entire room would be enveloped in a veil of black soot. It never occurred to anybody that during the forthcoming mass exterminations this was to be the SS staff headquarters.

There was great activity also in the whitewashed farmhouse, separated from the camp of Birkenau by a wooded area which was now bunker 5. Who would have thought that this peaceful and homely cottage would once again be used to gas thousands upon thousands of people?

Towards the end of April 1944 there were increasing rumours of the imminent extermination of the Jews of Hungary. To us, the prisoners of the *Sonderkommando*, this terrible news came as a devastating blow. Were we once more to stand by and watch while more hundreds upon thousands were done away with? Once again we pressed the camp Resistance to give the signal for an uprising. However, they still refused to run risks. Once more we were fobbed off with the idea that the Red Army's advance would be certain to demoralize and disorganize the SS very soon. Only when the time was ripe, we were informed, would an uprising have any chance of success. When we argued that this attitude meant nothing more or less than that we would yet again be forced to cremate hundreds of thousands of people, we were given to understand that there was no saving these people anyhow.

These stalling tactics on the part of the Resistance leadership led us to have serious doubts as to whether their leaders were genuinely prepared to fight and make sacrifices not only for their own lives but for the sake of saving umpteen thousands of other human beings. By now we were convinced that, as they watched their own chances of survival increase hourly, they were less and less inclined to jeopardize their own lives in an undertaking fraught with risks. Who could blame them for this attitude when liberation had come within their grasp? Thus we had no choice but to grit our teeth and wait for things to happen. Isolated as we were in the *Sonderkommando*, we did not, perhaps, appreciate that the Resistance felt responsible, first and foremost, for the camp as a whole, and that to its members to sacrifice individual groups seemed unavoidable.

At the beginning of May 1944 camp *Lagerkommandant* Höss arrived, followed a few days later by *Hauptscharführer* Moll. We knew Moll only too well, for it was he who had supervised the burning of the corpses which, in the summer of 1942, had risen to the earth's surface from their mass graves, and who, afterwards, had liquidated to the last man the *Sonderkommando* workers employed there. We were therefore seized by fear and foreboding at the sight of him. It was no doubt because of the vast scale of the forthcoming extermination enterprise that Höss had decided to place the death factories under new management and to entrust *Hauptscharführer* Moll, one of World War 2's worst murderers, with the post of manager.

Moll was rather short and thick-set. His chubby face was, as is often the case with gingery-blond people, covered with freckles. He wore a glass eye. In the *Sonderkommando* we used to call him 'Cyclops'. Moll was cruel, brutal and unscrupulous. For him Jews were sub-human creatures and he treated them accordingly. Anything was permitted when dealing with a *Rassenfeind*, a member of the hated race. He gloated over the suffering to which he submitted his victims and constantly thought up new torments and novel methods of torture. His sadism, his callousness, his bloodthirstiness and his lust to kill knew no bounds. He was an unpredictable monster whose state of mind was wholly unfathomable. Next to his unscrupulousness and fanaticism, he was also a man of indefatigable energy, petty conscientiousness and outstanding organizing ability, qualities which predestined this monstrous extermination maniac like no other to prepare and implement the biggest mass extermination undertaking of all time. In the opinion of the camp authorities *Oberscharführer* Voss was obviously not competent to cope with this task, and was therefore relieved of his post.

To begin with, Moll made many changes among the SS *Unterführer*s. *Unterscharführer* Steinberg was temporarily put in charge of crematoria 2 and 3. Very soon, however, he was relieved by *Oberscharführer* Muhsfeld who came from Majdanek. Soviet prisoners of war who had come to know him there told us what a merciless and brutal slave-driver this man with a harmless countenance and almost frail build really was. Under him worked *Rottenführer*s Holländer and Eidenmüller. Both were lean and lanky. Bunker 5 was under the management of *Unterscharführer* Eckardt. He was about twenty-eight, tall, slim and blond. Born in Hungary, he spoke Hungarian like his mother tongue. His crony, Kell, who came from Lodz, spoke Polish as well as Yiddish. Both had instructions to listen carefully to what victims said on their last walk to the place of extermination, in particular to watch out for the least signs of insubordination. Reinforcement for crematoria 4 and 5 – up to then mainly under the command of *Unterscharführer* Gorges and *Sturmmann* Kurschuss – came in the persons of *Unterscharführer* Seitz and, a little later, *Scharführer* Busch.

Soon after his arrival Moll ordered the excavation of five pits behind crematorium 5, not far from the three gas chambers. An increasing number of prisoners was also employed on the site near bunker 5 to dig more pits there. Here as well as at the crematorium yards wattle screens had been put up to prevent the curious from looking in at the death factories from the outside. The meadow behind the yard of crematorium 5, where thousands of spring flowers were in bloom, now turned into a strange building site where some 150 prisoners were set to work. Vast supplies of shovels, spades, wheelbarrows, timber, pneumatic drills and other tools, waited ready to be used for excavating cremation pits, once the surveying work was completed. Accompanied by his henchmen, extermination expert Moll paced up and down the large site, giving instructions for the siting of pits, a fuel depot, the spot where the ashes were to be crushed, and all the rest of the devices which he had thought up for the extermination and obliteration of human beings.

We were divided into five work teams. Urged on by constant threats and blows we now began to dig the sticky clay soil. Once again we had to yield to force and participate in the building of places which were to make possible the worst and most cruel mass murder yet at Auschwitz. No sooner had we begun our excavations than Moll's eagle eyes noticed that somebody had dug his spade into the clay a few centimetres beyond the taut marking string. At once he went berserk and began to shout: 'You bloody lot of idiots, are you blind? One more mistake like that and I'll show you! I demand accuracy and absolute obedience!' Encouraged by this outburst the rest of our persecutors felt it incumbent upon themselves to follow his example. A hail of blows rained down on us, accompanied by shouts of: 'Get on with it, you scum, come on, come on! We'll teach you how to do a day's work!' The *Kapo*s, too, began to yell at us, but at least they did not beat anyone.

There seemed to be no end to the rush and hurry of this first day on the building site; the pace of work grew more and more hectic as the day went on. The soil which we had dug out was loaded on to wheelbarrows and, under the watchful eyes of our tormentors, wheeled away at the double. Everything had to be done at the double. As for Moll, he was positively ubiquitous. Anywhere and at any time he was likely to pounce on people. The only thing that pleased him was the sight of us prisoners working ourselves to a frazzle. He was clearly fascinated by the filthy and barbarous business of murder which he had started: to bring it to a successful conclusion had become his life's work. But for us the day was dragging on. As the sun drew near to the horizon we felt our strength flagging. The strains of the camp orchestra greeting the returning work teams had long since faded away. But Moll made us go on working until it was dark. Then at last he blew his whistle, the sign for us to stop work. Spades were cleaned and put away; then we lined up in rows of five to be counted, first by the *Kapo*s and then by the SS to make sure no one was missing. And only then were we allowed to march back to camp. We were forcibly struck by the realization that things would be very different now that Moll was here.

As long as Voss was in charge of the crematoria, our living conditions had been relatively tolerable, in marked contrast to the brutal harshness of Moll. Of course, Voss too, was a murderer, but not the worst in Auschwitz by a long chalk. He was in his mid-thirties, of medium height and stocky, with a small, slightly hooked nose. Alcohol played an important part in his life. In the execution of his duties Voss displayed neither the fanaticism nor the zeal of Moll. Of course, he too was perfectly aware of his role as the man appointed to implement the mass murders. However, more than once during executions I heard him mutter 'Orders are orders': it was as though he wanted to dismiss any last scruples or give himself courage. His training in the SS had turned him into an uncritical and willing tool rather than a fanatically cruel exterminator. Voss had two personalities. He could be high-spirited, laughing and joking and talking about trivial things, even to us prisoners. Towards the SS men under his command he was rather affable and lenient, never standing on his dignity as the superior leader. On the other hand, he never batted an eyelid when it came to shooting men, women and children one after the other, if that was what he had to do. To us he was, in spite of everything, of all the executioners the least inhuman.

In addition to his penchant for alcohol, Voss had another weakness which we readily exploited, namely for gold, diamonds, dollars and other valuables. Since, after each gassing large amounts of these things were invariably picked up by prisoners detailed to search the corpses for hidden valuables, we managed to slip him quite a few of them. For example, shortly before each home-leave, diamonds of more than ordinary brilliance would be discreetly sewn into concealed places of his uniform by one of our tailors, without Voss incurring any risk whatever, needless to say. Any time he hinted more or less casually that he was due for leave soon, he would be told: 'But, *Herr Oberscharführer*, surely you don't intend to go on leave wearing this uniform jacket. Leave it here for the tailor to repair and press.' Of course, this was all put on and well Voss knew it. However, he pretended and so did we. This kind of corruption which we practised also with other members of the SS was a great help to us. As long as it involved no risk for them, many would, on occasion, turn a blind eye: many things went on which they did not, or did not want, to see. It was in this way that we managed to smuggle in the three hand-grenades, and also to make contact with a few of the outside teams, mainly with Russian prisoners of war who, at great risk, supplied us with arms and ammunition. To get them, we too needed gold, dollars and diamonds.

Under Moll our living conditions immediately deteriorated. He ruled us with a rod of iron, with the result that we were all steeped in despair and despondency. We doubted whether we would still be able to keep up our contact with the camp or to continue our plotting. Worse still, it was feasible that, by their brutal and vicious methods, Moll and his henchmen might succeed in reducing us all to *Mussulmans*, another reason to keep on pressing the Resistance for an early signal to rise up.

We could not understand why the civilized world allowed the death mills of Auschwitz to turn faster and faster without any discernible reaction, while the military overthrow of the Third Reich was agreed to by every right-thinking person. Almost a month had passed since the flight of Alfred Wetzler and Walter Rosenberg-Vrba, and there was no sign that they had reached any of their goals. Had the Nazis and their artful Propaganda Minister managed once again to deceive the rest of the world, we wondered. Could it be possible that their accounts were not believed because the crimes they had described were so ghastly as to be unbelievable? The two might even have been declared mentally ill and rushed into a psychiatric hospital, for had they not asserted that hundreds of thousands of human beings had been and were being murdered by means of a chemical compound used for pest control, merely because they were Jews?

Next morning we went to work in the knowledge that a general uprising was planned for a few weeks hence. This was the result of a conference between our own leaders and contacts of the camp Resistance. This news somewhat calmed most of us: we were now determined to avoid any conflict with our tormentors.

Even before work began Moll paced nervously up and down the site. He inspected the area, going from place to place, consulting a large drawing which he had unfolded and comparing it with smaller detailed drawings of the pits as well as of the rest of the extermination installations. Eagerly following in his wake were *Unterführer*s Eckhardt, Kell, Steinberg and Gorges, and *Sturmmann* Kurschuss, to all of whom he explained the tasks he expected to be carried out this day, while his Alsatian, on whom he doted, walked to heel.

Meanwhile the *Kapo*s stood by their teams waiting for their orders. A whistle and a brisk command made them sprint over to Moll and stand to attention in a row. When our *Kapo* returned he informed us that according to Moll's calculations five pits must be dug in one week. He had even worked out exactly how much earth would require moving each day.

We set to work. It was still cold, for the sun had not yet risen. Nobody had the least notion whether or how Moll's order could be carried out in this short time. To the accompaniment of threats from the SS and shouts of encouragement from the *Kapos* we went on digging the heavy clay. But the deeper we dug the harder the work became. After a few hours we were all thoroughly exhausted and near the end of our strength. When Moll's minions noticed that the pace of work was slowing down they belaboured us with their sticks yelling: 'Come on, come on, you lazy bastards, get a move on, faster!'

It was a good job Moll was nowhere near. The thought of the fiendish tortures which he knew how to use like no other man kept us in a constant state of fear and terror. When late that afternoon we heard the sound of his motor cycle and saw him roaring up, with his Alsatian sitting in the side-car, we felt distinctly uneasy. However, for once our fears were unfounded. After Moll had thoroughly inspected all the pits he ordered us to return to camp.

After a few days even Moll's henchmen had to admit that work on the pits could not be finished in the time allotted. For in the meantime it had started to rain and we were now standing ankle-deep in sticky, slippery clay. It was decided that we should concentrate all our efforts on two pits only. A few days later we made it: the two pits were 40 to 50 metres long, about 8 metres wide and 2 metres deep. However, this particular place of torment was not yet ready for use by any means. Once the rough work was finished, there followed the realization of the refinements thought up by the arch-exterminator's warped ingenuity.

Together with his assistant, Eckardt, he climbed down into the pit and marked out a 25 centimetres by 30 centimetres wide strip, running lengthways down the middle from end to end. By digging a channel which sloped slightly to either side from the centre point, it would be possible to catch the fat exuding from the corpses as they were burning in the pit, in two collecting pans at either end of the channel.

A group of prisoners had to climb down into the pit. Provided with spades, shovels, hammers, trowels, bricks, cement and spirit levels it was intended that they should make a drain channel for human fat. The whole concept seemed quite inconceivable: a drain channel to catch human fat which in turn was to be used as fuel in order to obliterate as fast as possible all traces of these murderous deeds. Outraged and depressed we saw the tragedy in all its horrendous scale coming ever closer.

There was still no sign from the outside world, while we were helpless in the face of SS power. Any refusal to work, even the merest hint, would have meant certain death without the slightest effect on the course of events.

Two more Jewish prisoners, Czeslaw Mordowicz and Arnost Rosin, managed to escape towards the end of May. Once again I supplied them with details including those of the extermination of Hungarian Jews which was then in full swing. Perhaps *they* would succeed in rousing world opinion.

When Moll had finished giving precise instructions concerning the digging of the channels he departed. Mercifully this time I did not have to work on 'technical installations', but was ordered to remove earth in wheelbarrows instead. A few hours later Moll returned. He walked straight up to one of the pits, climbed nimbly down and ran purposefully towards the centre. There he stopped, looking expectantly to the right and to the left along the channel. Then he ordered a couple of buckets of water to be brought. Before long they were lowered on ropes and placed in front of Moll. He took hold of the first bucket and poured water down one side of the channel, tensely watching its course. I peered down curiously from the top; from what I saw I knew at once that we were in serious trouble. The water, even before it reached the collecting pan at the front end of the pit, slopped back and slowly came to a halt. All eyes were on Moll; the tension was almost unbearable. When he realized that something was wrong with the fall of the channel he grabbed the empty bucket and brought it down on the heads of any prisoners unfortunate enough to be standing within reach. The *Kommandoführer*s, feeling the need to emulate their superior, leapt into the pit and pelted anyone in their way. Moll too flung himself on the wretched prisoners in the pit who were cowering together with fright and kicked them viciously, shouting at the top of his voice: 'You stupid shits, what's the matter with you, can't you even manage a simple job like that?'

Meanwhile evening had come. All the other work teams were back in camp. Only our team was in for a long night. At nightfall floodlights were set up. Moll put on blue overalls and gave a hand himself, along with Eckardt. With a long surveyor's rod, a water-level and other tools he estimated the incline all along the channel and superintended the alterations that were necessary.

When the work was finally finished, Moll again ordered a couple of buckets of water to be brought, seized the first one impatiently and again flung the water into the drainage channel. Then he stayed motionless for a few seconds, bending forward, and watched intently as it splashed down the channel. The process was repeated a couple of times, until the last bucket of water had been poured in the opposite direction along the channel. Now Moll ran irritably to the collecting pan at the front end of the pit and noted with satisfaction that this time the water had drained away completely and collected in the pan. Then he went calmly to the other collecting pan on the opposite side and there too he convinced himself of the success of his experiment. Now he relaxed. His face showed satisfaction and round his lips hovered something like a fleeting smile. He was obviously relieved, and convinced that he had taken a big step forward on the road towards a solution of his task.

But there was still one last vestige of doubt as to whether this extermination plant of his would really work in the way he had intended. I heard him ask Eckardt: 'What d'you think, will it work the same with hot fat as with water? Fat is viscous, isn't it?'

'I should think it will be all right, *Herr Hauptscharführer*,' replied his *Unterführer*, in an attempt to put his chief's mind at rest, although not altogether succeeding. Moll continued to stand there pondering and staring down into the pit without, however, uttering a word. We stood around, utterly exhausted and waiting. It was past midnight when Moll at last gave orders for us to return to camp.

After only a few hours' sleep a new day began and with it final preparations for the extermination campaign about to begin. The two new pits had considerably increased the capacity of the four crematoria at Birkenau. It was just a matter of adding the finishing touches. There was a constant stream of trucks delivering materials of all kinds, such as old railway sleepers, conifer branches, waste wood, beams, rags, large quantities of wood alcohol, barrels of waste lubricating oil, rammers, coarse- and fine-meshed iron sieves, cement, wooden planks, boards and barrels of chlorinated lime. Wherever the fuel was stacked in the open, it was roofed over.

It was the middle of May 1944 when the first transports of Hungarian Jews arrived in Birkenau. By now the *Sonderkommando* had been increased to 450 men, a number soon to be almost doubled. At the time when the machinery of extermination was running at full speed there were about 450 Hungarian, 200 Polish,

180 Greek, 3 Slovak and 5 German Jews as well as 19 Russian prisoners of war, 5 Polish prisoners in 'preventive custody' and one *Reichsdeutscher Kapo.*

Three more cremation pits were dug in the back yard of crematorium 5, making up the five Moll had ordered. In addition, the farmhouse which had served as a place of extermination in 1942, was put in running order. Its four rooms served as gas chambers while an additional four cremation pits were dug outside. The changing rooms were located in three wooden barracks, and the whole complex was known as bunker 5.

There were now nine of these large pits in addition to the crematorium ovens, making it possible to burn an almost unlimited number of corpses. All these installations originated in the brain of mass murderer Moll who had succeeded in turning a small corner of the earth's surface into something of such unspeakable vileness that it made Dante's *Inferno* appear like a pleasure garden.

From the outset the camp authorities took rigorous care to obliterate all traces of their crimes. For this reason the ashes of the burnt corpses were thrown into fishponds or the river Vistula. In this connection Moll had thought up a new technique to expedite the removal of ashes. He ordered an area next to the pits adjoining crematorium 5 and measuring about 60 metres by 15 metres to be concreted; on this surface the ashes were crushed to a fine powder before their final disposal.

At the time this concreting work was in progress, the liquidation of Hungarian Jewry was in full swing. It seems incredible that eleven months before the end of the war it was possible for long trains to travel constantly back and forth between Hungary and Birkenau when one would have thought they were urgently required for the war effort. Almost daily several trains consisting, on average, of forty to fifty cattle trucks, arrived on the newly built ramp at Birkenau. The trucks into which up to 100 people had been crammed were bolted; they were unlocked only when the train had reached its destination. The people were parched with thirst since, during their journey lasting several days, they had been given not a drop of water. Many died *en route* from the rigours of the journey.

Long columns of those who during the selections had been chosen for the walk to the gas chambers struggled along the dusty roads, exhausted and in low spirits, mothers pushing prams, taking the older children by the hand. The young helped and supported the old and sick. Some had strayed into this procession because on the ramp they had implored the SS not to separate them from their frail and helpless relatives; how were they to know that only hours later their relatives would require no more help.

The road from the ramp to the gas chambers led past long barbed-wire fences. Behind them the victims walking to their death could see emaciated figures in zebra-striped prison garb, moving about apathetically. Those who arrived at night looked into the glare of thousands of lamps spreading over the lifeless landscape a pale and ghostly light, the sombre effect enhanced by the SS guards on their watch-towers with their machine-guns at the ready. So bleak was the sight which met new arrivals day or night that somehow it plunged them into a state of apathy. In addition they were invariably plagued by raging thirst, particularly during the summer heat, and the thought of water so preoccupied them that they seemed no longer able to think of anything else or of paying more than the most cursory attention to the unusual surroundings in which they found themselves.

This was precisely the physical and mental state of those 2,000-odd people who, at dawn one hot June day in 1944, arrived in the front yard of crematorium 5. From there between two lines formed by SS men they were herded into the near-by grove. And now their fate was finally sealed; for here, within the shadow of the crematorium and its three gas chambers there was no escape.

They were standing some hundred metres from the pits, their view blocked by a 3-metres high camouflage screen; a few SS guards, their rifles at the ready, were posted in front of the screen to prevent anyone from going too close and through the gaps stealing a glance at the inferno behind it. For behind the screen raged the fire of hell. Crackling, hissing and sizzling it flared up into the sky like a giant torch, covering the area with a diffuse, murky-black cloud.

But the imagination of the people could not possibly envisage that the smoke clouding the sun, the huge fire raging behind the screen and the sickly smell polluting the air came from the burning of thousands of murdered human beings who, only a few hours earlier, had suffered the fate now awaiting them. That morning they were made to wait their turn for the gas chamber since the victims of the previous night had not yet been cleared away. Every now and then *Hauptscharführer* Moll put in an appearance, asking people to be patient and promising that soon they would be given something to drink.

Since last night three transports had disappeared into the gas chambers of crematorium 5. As soon as every last body had been flung on the heap behind the crematorium, the next batch of victims was led into the changing room to undress, the clothes left behind by their predecessors having been whisked away first. All this took time, hence the waiting period in the grove for those who arrived later. Meanwhile Moll and his minions, anxious to have the gas chambers cleared and superficially cleaned, harried and hurried the exhausted bearers.

Moll returned once more to the grove and explained to the waiting crowd that now it really would not be long before they were given a drink. Several of the people were so desperately thirsty that they crouched on the ground licking the dew-wet grass. When the long-promised drink failed to materialize the people began to grow restless, distressed above all by the piteous cries and entreaties of their children who were begging their mothers for just a few drops of water. Some of the women sidled up to the SS guards, cautiously getting near enough for their voices to be heard, and began desperately to plead with them for water. The guards pointed their rifles at them and with threatening gestures forced the women to retreat.

Next to appear was *Unterscharführer* Eckardt who talked to the crowd in Hungarian. He, too, tried to subdue their restlessness, promising them something to drink soon. Of course, he knew very well that hope and the will to live would once more stir in these people if they were allowed to quench their burning thirst. This pre-programmed suffering was deliberately aimed at paralysing the ability to notice things and the will to resist in order to allow the giant machinery of murder to run smoothly and at full speed. Not a minute must be lost, otherwise the plan to liquidate several hundred thousand Jews within a few weeks might not succeed. In Moll's strategy of extermination the reduction of vital energies by prolonged thirst played a carefully planned and psychologically important part.

The whistle of a train engine, the scream of wheels, the hiss of steam escaping from the valves, and the loud shriek of brakes, indicated that yet another transport had come up to the ramp. Some time later a crowd dragged itself along, wearily surging to and fro on the camp road. There was a confused sound of many voices, weeping, and children's cries, above which rose shouts of command and curses. The procession stopped in front of section B2f and waited there until their predecessors, who were waiting in the little wood, had been herded into the gas chambers of crematorium 5.

The floor of the backyard of crematorium 5 was littered with amorphous heaps of corpses. One after the other the bodies were dragged out by the bearers who placed them side by side on their backs in a long row where their teeth were removed, their body orifices searched for hidden valuables, and the hair of the women cut off. Only then were the corpses released for cremation.

As it began to grow light, the fire was lit in two of the pits in which about 2,500 dead bodies lay piled one on top of the other. Two hours later all that could be discerned in the white-hot flames were countless charred and scorched shapes, their blackish-phosphorescent hue a sign that they were in an advanced stage of cremation. At this point the fire had to be kept going from outside because the pyre which at first protruded about half a metre above the edge of the pit had, in the meantime, gone below this level. While in the crematorium ovens, once the corpses were thoroughly alight, it was possible to maintain a lasting red heat with the help of fans, in the pits the fire would burn only as long as the air could circulate freely in between the bodies. As the heap of bodies settled, no air was able to get in from outside. This meant that we stokers had constantly to pour oil or wood alcohol on the burning corpses, in addition to human fat, large quantities of which had collected and was boiling in the two collecting pans on either side of the pit. The sizzling fat was scooped out with buckets on a long curved rod and poured all over the pit causing flames to leap up amid much crackling and hissing. Dense smoke and fumes rose incessantly. The air reeked of oil, fat, benzole and burnt flesh.

During the day-shift there were, on average, 140 prisoners working in and round crematoria 4 and 5. Some twenty-five bearers were employed in clearing the gas chamber and removing the corpses to the pits. Ten dental mechanics and barbers had to wrench out gold teeth, search the bodies for valuables and cut off the women's hair. It was the job of another twenty-five bearers to stack the corpses in three layers on top of the fuel in the pits. About fifteen stokers had to place the fuel in the pit and to light and maintain the fire by constantly stoking in between the corpses and pouring oil, wood alcohol and liquid human fat over them. There were approximately thirty-five men in the ash team. Some had to dig the ashes from the pits and remove them to the ash depot. The others were busy pulverizing the ashes. A smaller group of prisoners loaded clothing, shoes and other of the victims' belongings on trucks, to be taken to *Canada*; this group also fetched food for the midday meal from the camp kitchen and did any other odd jobs. The remaining prisoners worked in crematorium 4, where operations went on 'normally'.

This basic organization of work was changed frequently, especially when additional hands were wanted elsewhere. Thus it often happened that some of the stokers were ordered into the crematorium at short notice to help with the clearing of the changing room or with removing corpses. There were similar arrangements for the night-shift. Not infrequently the stoker team was reduced to half its number because fires could not be lit at night on account of black-out regulations.

In order to prepare the third pit for cremation old railway sleepers, wooden beams, planks, and sawdust were arranged in layers and covered with a layer of dry fir branches. Then the bearers laid about 400 corpses face upwards in four long rows on top of the fuel. The next layer again consisted of fuel covered, as before, with fir branches. Then followed another layer of corpses. This sequence was repeated once more until, in the end, there were some 1,200 dead bodies in three layers. Meanwhile the stokers had soaked pieces of material and rags in oil and wood alcohol and stuffed them in between the fuel in many places. Then they thrust long burning torches deep into the pit. These torches consisted of iron poles with handles at one end, while wound round the other were oil-soaked rags. All this work had to be carried out double-quick, to the incessant goading and invective of the SS. Soon in many places in the pit there rose small columns of smoke. The fire spread quickly and before long it began to crackle and crepitate. When the rags and tatters in the pit caught alight there were puffs of smoke like little explosions. Acrid smoke and fumes spread in thickening clouds over the landscape of death.

From time to time *Hauptscharführer* Moll in his incongruous white uniform appeared at the pits to make sure that everything was going like clock-work, a high order adorning his chest. It was, so I was told, the *Kriegsverdienstkreuz* with swords. No doubt it had been bestowed upon him by his *Führer* for his unceasing and selfless service in the extermination camp of Birkenau. It was an 'honour', I understand, awarded to very few. Whenever Moll showed his face his SS underlings, who were drunk most of the time, increased their yelling and goading. It was as if they wanted to demonstrate that in this appalling business in which they were engaged they had just as few scruples as their chief. *Unterscharführers* Gorges and Busch, on the other hand, were more restrained and never went beyond what was absolutely expected of them, not even in Moll's presence.

The SS guards on their watch-towers beyond the barbed wire which encircled the area round the pits were, without exception, older men. It was obvious that they were badly upset by the ghoulish spectacle. I often wondered what went on in the minds of these men of advanced years as from their eyries they observed the diabolical events below.

The corpses in the pit looked as if they had been chained together. Tongues of a thousand tiny blue–red flames were licking at them. The fire grew fiercer and flames leapt higher and higher. Under the ever-increasing heat a few of the dead began to stir, writhing as though with some unbearable pain, arms and legs straining in slow motion, and even their bodies straightening up a little, hesitant and with difficulty, almost as if with their last strength they were trying to rebel against their doom. Eventually the fire became so fierce that the corpses were enveloped by flames. Blisters which had formed on their skin burst one by one. Almost every corpse was covered with black scorch marks and glistened as if it had been greased. The searing heat had burst open their bellies: there was the violent hissing and spluttering of frying in great heat. Boiling fat flowed into the pans on either side of the pit. Fanned by the wind, the flames, dark-red before, now took on a fiery white hue: the corpses were burning so fiercely that they were consumed by their own heat. The process of incineration took five to six hours. What was left barely filled a third of the pit. The shiny whitish-grey surface was strewn with countless skulls.

Now prisoners of the ash team, whose job was surely the worst of all, went to work. To begin with the white-hot ashes were sprayed with water to cool down the surface. Immediately a cloud of hot steam rose enveloping the pits and everything around them in a sticky grey mist. Whenever a jet of water hit one of the skulls it instantly disintegrated. As soon as the ashes had cooled down a little, wooden metal-covered boards were thrown into the pit. Prisoners of the ash team climbed down and began to shovel out the still hot ashes. Although their mittens and berets gave them some make-shift protection, hot ashes kept blowing down on them, especially when it was windy, causing severe facial burns and eye injuries, sometimes even blindness, so that after a short time they were issued with protective goggles.

Once the pits had been emptied and the ashes taken to the ash depot, they were piled up in man-high heaps. However, in these heaps there were many limbs and other parts of bodies not completely burnt. With special forks charred fingers, hands, remains of arms, legs and feet, and also of trunks, were fished out and burnt a second time in a smaller pit. The rest of the ashes were then pulverized on the concrete slab, thoughtfully provided for this purpose by Moll, by first being pounded and then passed through different-meshed sieves. In those days there were not enough trucks to deal with the giant mountains of ashes. For this reason special pits were dug, filled with these ashes and then covered over.

The prisoners employed in this work were almost without exception Greek Jews. As they stamped the ashes they accompanied their monotonous activity by non-stop cheerful singing. Both stamping and singing were constantly drowned by the shrieking of an electric circular saw cutting up the firewood for the pits. The wooden beams used for this purpose arrived in open goods waggons coupled to the transport trains, several of which arrived almost daily. The victims standing on the ramp and seeing the long square wooden beams might have speculated that they were intended for use as building material. Little did they know that a few hours later they might well be used to cremate their own bodies. On several occasions I was detailed to work with the team taking these beams from the ramp to the place where the circular saw stood. Another team with which I worked was taken by truck to the woods where, under heavy guard, they had to collect fir branches and brushwood.

The people who that morning had stood waiting in the little wood were a few hours later driven into the three gas chambers of crematorium 5. While the body carriers dragged the dead outside, a new crowd of people was already waiting, unsuspecting, in the wood. They were young men, who had arrived in the course of the morning and had been made to wait on the camp road by section Bₐf until their predecessors had been taken to the gas chambers. They, too, had to wait patiently till all the dead had been taken out of the gas chambers and the items left in the changing room had been removed.

The first of several trucks that took these things to the belongings store, *Canada*, drove into the yard in front of the crematorium. The driver was careful to back the vehicle exactly in front of the double door from which a passageway led into the changing room. I, too, was sent there to work with a group of some fifteen prisoners to collect the clothes and belongings left behind by the victims. SS men were strictly forbidden to touch any of these things, no doubt to keep them from temptation of helping themselves to valuables belonging to *Rassenfeinden*, members of the enemy race. It was a temptation, however, which only few could resist. With the exception of Moll every SS man who worked in the crematorium area was keen on gold, diamonds and dollars. Each one tried to grab what he could.

But we were just as nimble-fingered. Stealing was an art we had learnt in the concentration camp: we needed to steal in order to survive. Since we were amply supplied with Hungarian salami, goose dripping, jam and cigarettes, we were able to use any valuables we *organized* to buy arms and ammunition.

Heaps of clothes lay strewn all over the concrete floor of the changing room, the Stars of David like a drift of yellow flowers on the ground. No SS man was in sight, so I joined the other prisoners in a rapid search among the clothes lying about. To be sure one had to be on one's guard all the time, for woe betide anyone who was caught by Moll with gold, diamonds or dollars: he was a goner. The inevitable death sentence always had a prelude which Moll thought up to suit the occasion and which in cruelty and perverted sadism had no equal. There was one wretched prisoner on whom Moll, during a spot check, found several dollar bills. From his wide range of sadistic punishment he selected one which he was certain would have the desired effect as a deterrent. He took the prisoner to one of the pits where the top layer of ashes was still red-hot. At the edge of the pit Moll drew his pistol and remarked cynically: 'I ought to shoot you, you fucking Yid. But I'm not like that, I'll give you a chance. I'll let you go if you run barefoot across the pit twice.' Hoping desperately to save his life, the boy took off his shoes and leapt into the pit. In vain he tried to run for his life: as he collapsed into the red-hot embers Moll gave him the *coup de grâce*.

Moll had a morbid partiality for obscene and salacious tortures. Thus it was his wont to turn up in the crematorium when the victims were taking off their clothes. Like a meat inspector he would stride about the changing room, selecting a couple of naked young women and hustling them to one of the pits where corpses were being burnt. Faced with the sight of this pit of hell the women were distracted. They stood at the edge of the pit, rooted to the spot, gazing fixedly at the gruesome scene at their feet. Moll who was watching them closely got a tremendous kick out of their terror. In the end he shot them from behind so that they fell forward into the burning pit.

Once I saw several young women faced with this situation who fled like shy deer and made for the barbed-wire fence. At once Moll set his Alsatian on them. The dog bounded after them, chasing them hither and thither and snapping at their legs and buttocks. Meanwhile Moll's assistants, Eckardt, Kell and Kurschuss, came running and with their truncheons drove the terrified women back to the pit which was still burning fiercely. There Moll was eagerly waiting to satisfy his thirst for blood. He ordered the women to stand side by side facing the pit. The sight of the burning bodies struck renewed terror into them. Meanwhile Moll's specially trained Alsatian was loping back and forth about half a metre behind the wretched women; panting, his tail almost horizontal, his eyes glittering, he watched for the least movement of his victims. The women, bleeding from wounds inflicted by the dog, stood petrified at the edge of the pit, their horrified eyes on the burning corpses. Moll was in his element. Sexually excited he shouted at the defenceless women: 'Just you look at that, look at it well! In a moment you'll burn exactly like them down there!' And then, from behind, he shot them one after the other, with a silenced carbine, and they fell forward into the inferno of the pit.

One day Moll discovered two gold rings on one of the young prisoners. He had the boy's hands tied behind his back; then he was hanged from a hook by his fettered hands. He fainted from the excruciating pain. Moll ordered him to be taken down and had a couple of buckets of water thrown over him. When he came to and still refused to confess from where he received the rings Moll rushed out of the room shouting: 'I'll show you!' He returned carrying a tin of petrol which he poured all over the poor devil. Then he threw a lighted match at him. Like a living torch the boy ran shrieking towards the high-tension barbed wire, but before he could reach it Moll put him out of his misery with a well-aimed shot.

Intellectuals, a sizeable number of whom were members of the *Sonderkommando*, were among the frequent victims of Moll's perverted tortures. He seemed to have a knack for picking them out. When he had one of his sadistic turns, he would select his victims by approaching several prisoners and barking at them: 'What's your trade?' Almost invariably his hunch that he had sniffed out an intellectual was correct; he was very proud of this flair.

Another unusual entertainment in which he would indulge every now and then was called swim-frog. The unfortunate victims were forced into one of the pools near the crematoria where they had to swim around croaking like frogs until they drowned from exhaustion. Up to that moment Moll and his minions would stand there gloating over their victims' death struggle. The least attempt to get near the edge of the water-filled pit was foiled by a pistol or gun being thrust into the prisoner's face.

Yet another game in Moll's repertoire was one called brick-bashing. He divided his chosen victims into two teams. Each prisoner was given two bricks, one for each hand, which he had to bang together until the bricks were shattered. Of course every one who took part in this 'competition' sustained painful and bleeding injuries. The prisoners of the losing team were made to run against the barbed wire, but before they reached it, Moll would bag them like so many hares. Another thing he was fond of doing was to kill babies by flinging them live into the boiling human fat on either side of the pits.

But whenever the *Lagerkommandant* or any other high-ranking SS leader turned up, Moll managed to pull himself together and everything in the death factory went as usual without extravagant excesses.

There were many reasons why for us the *organizing* of valuables was absolutely vital. Without valuables it would have been impossible to plan an uprising, support the Resistance, corrupt the SS, get more arms and ammunition, and many other things. At the same time our leaders, although they had high hopes for the successful outcome of the uprising, made contingency plans in the event of failure. To ensure that posterity would learn of the events at Auschwitz and Birkenau, a few prisoners prepared a handwritten account of the *Sonderkommando* which was placed in tins and buried, in the hope that perhaps one day they might be found.

We went through the clothing with the agility of pickpockets, beginning with the inside pockets. These would produce wallets, identity cards, passports, school reports, university diplomas, family photographs, among other things. In the outside pockets we found combs, pencils, matches, cigarettes, glasses, pills, French letters, and handkerchiefs. But we were even more interested in certain places where valuables were usually either sewn in or concealed. It was mainly the collars and padded shoulders of men's suits which we probed nimbly and with care. If there was a rustling noise or if we felt something hard, we would undo the seams with sharp pocket-knives. As a rule this produced dollar bills or diamonds. Once the clothes had been checked, we gave a quick going-over to the bundles. They contained toothbrushes, toothpaste, sweaters, stockings, toys, knives, forks, spoons, candles, in other words, the sort of things which people who were supposed to be going to the East for resettlement might consider useful for their future daily lives. It was interesting to note that despite the summer's heat most of the deported had taken care to provide for the following winter. There were winter coats and also many costly furs, positive proof that the Jews from Hungary neither knew nor suspected their ultimate destination to be the gas chamber.

Since the previous night 10,000 people had perished in the three gas chambers of crematorium 5 alone, while on the site of bunker 5 with its four gas chambers corpses were burnt in four pits. In addition, in crematoria 2, 3 and 4 with a total of five gas chambers and thirty-eight ovens work went on at full speed. Taking this kind of 'plant capacity' into consideration it will be readily understood how it was possible to exterminate about 400,000 Hungarian Jews within a few weeks.

In order to transport 10,000 people from Hungary to Birkenau about 100 railway carriages were needed. It needed only a few trucks to take their ashes to the Vistula.

At this time, rumours began to circulate concerning contingency plans by the camp administration in case of a surprise advance by the Soviet army. These plans, so it was whispered, included arrangements for the rapid liquidation of all prisoners. As these rumours increased, they began to alarm even those in the Resistance who, convinced that they themselves would survive, had up to now turned their backs on demands for a general uprising. It was an open secret that *Hauptscharführer* Moll had been entrusted with drawing up this contingency plan. Nobody knew what this plan was, and only after the war it was learned that he had proposed to bring up an SS artillery regiment which was to fire at the camp from all sides. Simultaneously a group of aeroplanes was to bombard the camp.

With this threat of imminent danger hanging over us, a Friday in mid-June was fixed as the time for the uprising. It was agreed with the Resistance that all was to go according to our previously arranged plan.

The four crematoria and bunker 5 were situated at the end of the two central access routes in Birkenau, west of B1 and B3 the sections under construction. From a strategic aspect they were probably the most advantageous starting points for the uprising which was based on the following plan. In the late afternoon, before the return of the work teams, the *SS-Unterführer*s as well as the SS guards on the site of crematoria 4 and 5 were to be overpowered and their arms and uniforms seized. Their bodies were to be burnt immediately in one of the pits in order to cover all traces. This first step did not appear to present many problems; for there were 140 of us facing only seven SS men. There were, it is true, among us many who could not be expected to take an active part; nevertheless we were so superior in numbers that the first surprise blow could not, in fact, go wrong.

It was further planned that the SS team on the site of crematoria 2 and 3 should be liquidated by the 180 prisoners who usually worked there. There would then be a waiting period until the night-shift was brought up by the *SS Unterführer*s, and the SS guards changed. On entering the crematorium site the SS escort party and the SS guards going on duty at the barbed wire near crematorium 5 were, like their predecessors, to be instantly overpowered, disarmed and their uniforms seized. If this second blow was successful we would possess more than twenty SS uniforms and as many fire-arms, among them several machine-guns. It had also been decided who was to play the role of uniformed SS men: all of them were strong, courageous and determined men, who spoke German fluently and were afraid of nothing; they were to play a decisive part in the further course of the rebellion. Some of them had been detailed to make a breach in the outer cordon in order to prepare the way to freedom. This cordon was manned by SS guards on watch-towers, armed with machine-guns. Shortly before evening roll-call and before the outer cordon was withdrawn three of our men, disguised as SS men, were to lead a 'work team' of ten prisoners to one of these watch-towers. To avoid suspicion these prisoners were to carry all manner of tools, thus creating the impression that they were moving out to work, albeit at an unusual hour. This was nothing out of the ordinary. When this 'work team' had arrived at the first watch-tower one of the fake SS men was to tell the guard that he had been ordered to carry out certain safety precautions. The guard was to be requested to come down for a short time. As he descended it would be easy to finish him off quietly with a silenced small-bore gun. This was important because we had at all costs to avoid arousing the suspicions of the neighbouring guard.

The plan was for further SS posts to be eliminated in like manner and in this way to create a wide escape corridor. This undertaking was to be supported by the work teams who worked beyond the outer cordon. It was their task to overpower their overseers before their return to camp, to disarm them and then to tackle the elimination of further SS posts on watch-towers along the outer cordon. After the overpowering of the SS men at the crematorium site the bulk of *Sonderkommando* prisoners, guarded by their comrades in SS disguise, were to return to camp as usual, in an orderly fashion. However, on the way every *SS-Blockführer* whose office they passed was to be shot. A stock of small-bore rifles was kept in the *Kommandoführers*' offices, and it would not be difficult to seize them once the SS men had been killed. Furthermore, on the way back to camp all telephone cables were to be cut.

A third group was to remain on the crematorium sites and wait for the start of the inevitable shoot-out with the SS as the signal for blowing up and setting fire to the crematorium buildings. All the remaining teams working inside the outer cordon had made similar plans for the overpowering and disarming of their guards. If things worked out we should have so many uniforms and fire-arms that it would be possible to force a break-out through the outer cordon. Prisoners left in the barrack areas were to set fire to the buildings. With insulated tin cutters they were to cut holes in the barbed-wire fences, large enough to allow people to pass through safely.

Those who were armed and in SS uniform were, first and foremost, to safeguard the escape of the rest, guarding the flight corridor on all sides against attacks until the majority of fleeing prisoners had passed through the outer cordon. Then and only then were they to follow on into the woods where the partisans would take them to safety. To avoid confusion during the battles with the SS it had been arranged that our men would identify themselves by wearing yellow armbands on their right sleeves.

If our flight succeeded we planned to join the partisans. We believed that through acts of sabotage, such as the blowing up of railway tracks, we might obstruct, or even prevent, further deportations.

All the preparations for the break-out had been completed, each one of us having been familiarized with his particular task. All the arms we possessed were in readiness including a supply of dynamite *organized* from the Union munitions factory in Auschwitz. All of us realized that only a few would survive the impending struggle.

When the crucial day arrived we were in a state of tense and nervous anticipation. Repeated signals that all was well were received from our contacts with the Resistance in the camp. Feverish with excitement we waited for the afternoon. I remembered the hopeless confusion on the occasion when that young dancer had grabbed Quackernack's pistol and shot *Unterführer* Schillinger dead. If one single pistol in the hands of a weak woman could create a panic among the SS, how would they react when faced with a number of armed prisoners determined to fight for their freedom? So full of suspense was the atmosphere that at first no one noticed the arrival, complete with wheelbarrow, of three prisoners from crematorium 2, under the pretext that we urgently required certain building materials. They informed our leaders that due to unforeseen circumstances jeopardizing its success the uprising had to be postponed quite suddenly.

We were absolutely stunned by this news. To begin with we simply could not take it in that at the last moment we had once again been thwarted. Declarations that it was a matter of only a few days' postponement did not help to reassure us either. All sorts of rumours were going round. One asserted that there had been difficulties in the *Canada* work team, another that the Katowice Gestapo had carried out an extensive swoop on the partisans. None of us ever found out the real reasons for calling off the uprising.

When the excitement had died down, our terrible monotonous routine ground on until one day towards the end of June 1944 our situation became still more critical. That cunning fox Moll had hit upon the idea of housing the entire *Sonderkommando* in the crematoria in order to put an end to our contact with the rest of the camp. Some of us made their quarters in the lofts of crematoria 2 and 3 while the majority, including myself, was billeted in the changing room of crematorium 4. At first we were completely stumped: this transfer cut right across our escape plans simply because we no longer returned to camp when going off duty. Hence new plans had to be made. I dared not think about what would happen if Moll now decided to carry out a selection among members of the *Sonderkommando*; I knew my chances would be nil. For it stood to reason that no prisoner with an 'old' number would be allowed to stay alive: we had seen and heard too much.

Once more our leaders were severely criticized not only by the radicals among us but this time also by the Soviet prisoners of war. Their situation had become precarious after an incident when one of them turned on a *Kommandoführer* who had hit him. When the Russian's companions came to his aid, the *Kommandoführer* indicated that he would have them all transferred, and they all knew from experience what that meant. That the threat was not carried out was due entirely to *Unterscharführer* Steinberg's intervention on their behalf.

One of the *Sonderkommando* workers was a Berlin Jew called Zander. This Zander was in some way related to Steinberg who had told him that he had nothing to fear as long as he, Steinberg, served in Birkenau. Everybody knew about the arrangement, and it was this which persuaded our *Kapo*, Kaminski, to approach Zander asking him to intervene with Steinberg concerning the Russians and their threatened transfer. Kaminski was anxious to calm our Russian fellow prisoners down and to restore harmony in the *Sonderkommando*. Zander managed to persuade his brother-in-law – or whatever Steinberg was – that the fisticuffs between the Russians and the *Kommandoführer* had not been insubordination but a single misdemeanour committed by someone the worse for drink. (Alcohol was *organized* either from the belongings of those who had been gassed or in exchange for diamonds, gold or other valuables by prisoners in the *Sonderkommando* who worked outside the camp and in contact with civilians.) Steinberg in his turn talked the *Kommandoführer* into forgetting about the whole incident.

Thus peace was once more restored. We were able to keep up contact with the Resistance in the camp: three times daily the ration carriers went into the camp where they had the opportunity of meeting prisoners in the Resistance. The hospital was another contact point. Shortly after our isolation on the crematorium site it became necessary to establish a small ward for prisoners requiring in-patient treatment. The ward, under the direction of Dr Pach, was set up because prisoners of the ash team continued to sustain severe burns for which they could not be treated as out-patients. We thought it absurd and contradictory for Moll to allow these prisoners to be treated and cared for, but then the laws of logic did not apply here. There were also different teams of artisans on our site whose presence helped to ease our isolation. One of these workmen was always ready to take messages to the Resistance and bring back their answers.

Once Dr Pach's ward for in-patients had been set up the treatment of *Sonderkommando* out-patients was taken over by Dr Bendel. He, too, was of great assistance in helping us to maintain contact with the camp: for instance, by making fictitious diagnoses he occasionally managed to have one of our Resistance leaders admitted to the camp hospital. Among the patients there were a few Soviet officers who were prisoners of war. Some of our people became quite friendly with these men and discussed with them our plan of escape which now needed rethinking on account of our being cut off from the camp. However, it turned out quite soon that we could stick to the basic plan: what mattered now was to overpower every SS man on the crematorium sites before their relief for the night-shift came on. By the time the SS on night-shift arrived, our chosen men would have to be in SS uniform; taking advantage of the initial confusion, they could then, with assistance from other prisoners, swiftly dispose of the arriving SS and seize their uniforms and arms. Then a number of us would form up as a work team and, under escort of our armed comrades in SS uniform, set out, ostensibly on our way back to camp. From then on the plan could remain as outlined above.

Meanwhile transports of Jews from Hungary continued to arrive on the ramp at Birkenau and to go to the gas chamber. In this hot summer of 1944 a large number of transports came from the labour camps of Radom and Pustkow, and from Greece, and there were another few thousand, mainly of Czech nationality.

However, Jews were not the only target of the Nazi extermination programme. In the spring of 1943 they had begun to deport to Auschwitz gypsies from European countries including Germany, France, Poland and Roumania. They were quartered in camp B2e, called the Gypsy Camp. There they lived, men, women and children, in wooden barracks under conditions which, in many respects, differed favourably from the rest of the camp. They were allowed to wear civilian clothes, their hair was not cut off, and they were not subjected to harassment or beatings. With few exceptions they were not used for work outside their own camp. On the other hand the result of this isolation was that they suffered more than the majority of prisoners from a constant shortage of food and disastrous hygienic conditions. Unable to move out of their camp, they were also unable to *organize* anything. The crowding together of a great many people – whose number was increasing steadily through new births – in so small a space, the lack of drugs, medicines, and food, added to the lack of hygiene, resulted in frequent illnesses often ending in death, particularly in new-born babies. There were a few Czech and Polish doctors who worked indefatigably among the sick gypsies. We, too, let them have what supplies of drugs and medicines we could obtain and spare, but none of it was more than a drop in the ocean.

In the crematorium we noticed that there was an increasing number of corpses from the Gypsy Camp, the majority of which were small children and elderly people. The latter were only skin and bones, almost all of them had scabies, and many of the dead children looked as though they had been gnawed at by rats. We were told by doctors that this was, in fact, a disease called noma which affects mainly debilitated children.

By August 1944 the Nazis had obviously decided to exterminate the *Artfremden*, or ethnically alien, gypsies. Before the gassings began, a large number of them were transferred to other camps; almost 3,000 people were left.

One late evening several trucks rolled into the yard of crematorium 5. Gypsies who had remained in section B2e and were to be gassed that night had been crammed into the cargo space. On the running-boards stood SS men who were accompanying the death convoy. When the vehicles stopped they jumped down and opened the tail-boards. The people – there were a lot, easily 300 in all – climbed out and were sent into the changing room along a corridor lined with armed SS guards. Meanwhile the trucks went back to transport more of the human cargo. After about twenty minutes a new convoy rolled up with more candidates for death. These people were also directed into the changing room, while the trucks went away again. The process was repeated two or three times more, until towards midnight over 1,000 people were in the changing room of crematorium 5. The rest had been put in crematorium 3. When the first batch was in the changing room several *SS-Unterführer*s arrived and asked the people to go right to the back and undress. Simultaneously SS men moved away from the door to the back part of the room and formed a sort of cordon in front of the crowd. After a time members of the SS brass also made their appearance, among them the *Kommandant* of Auschwitz II, Kramer; *Lagerführer* Schwarzhuber; some SS doctors; and other SS leaders. Even Moll, who led the extermination routine, ran busily around with his underlings, giving directions and orders.

Today a peculiar atmosphere reigned in the changing room. The gypsies who were to be gassed had known some of the SS men present for some time, and they tried to get into conversation with them as they usually did. In the course of time they had come to be on almost familiar terms with the SS. This was probably because most of them spoke German, and perhaps also because the SS men had had no plausible reason to hate them. Unlike the Jews, Bolsheviks, Slavs, and other 'sub-humans', the gypsies had never had many pronouncements of a compromising nature made against them by the official Nazi propaganda. Before coming here many of them had fought as German soldiers and had even been decorated. Perhaps their naturally optimistic view of life, which even in the camp did not prevent them from following their customs, for example playing music with passion and spirit, had played a part in making the SS men treat them more benevolently. But now in the changing room the SS men behaved in a cool and distant manner. When spoken to they remained silent and did not respond to questions and gestures. This took away the gypsies' last illusions. They guessed what was planned for them and once again stood up desperately to their fate.

Towards midnight the changing room was full of people. With every minute that passed the alarm increased. The room might have been a giant beehive. On all sides sounded cries of despair, lamentations, and reproachful accusations. Choruses of voices cried: 'We're German citizens! We've done nothing wrong!' Others shouted: 'We want to live! Why do you want to kill us?' There was another unusual thing, which I had never before witnessed in this ante-room of death. Numerous men were holding their wives in a tight embrace, pressed convulsively against them as if merged into one, passionately but despairingly making love for the last time. It was as if in this way they wanted to say farewell to the most precious thing they had in the world, but also to their own life.

One could see that most of the SS men had a bad conscience. They hadn't shown any scruples about annihilating Jews, the killing of whom was now a daily routine for all of them, yet they clearly found it unpleasant and distressing to help exterminate people with whom they had been on quite good terms up to now. But in this dismal place there was no room for sentiment. The extermination routine took its usual course. Moll and his helpers cocked their pistols and rifles and, in a way that allowed no misunderstanding, asked the people, who meanwhile had undressed, to leave the changing room at once and go into those three rooms in which they were to be gassed. As they took their last walk, many wept in despair, others crossed themselves and prayed to God, and yet others, who even now were unwilling to come to terms with their inevitable fate, turned to the SS men and, gesticulating wildly, shouted without stopping: 'We are German citizens! You can't do this to us!'

For a while desperate shouts and cries could be heard coming from the gas chambers until the gas had done its deadly work and choked the last voice.

Even before the opening of the chamber after the gassing, Moll ordered all prisoners to go immediately to the two rooms between the changing room and the gas chambers. There we were locked in, ostensibly because there had been an air-raid warning. This was nonsense, of course, since through the barred windows we could see that the camp lights had not been switched off. Quite obviously we were locked up under a pretext, a fact which made us feel distinctly uncomfortable. Perhaps our last hour had come. The muffled sounds of two shots were ominous. Much to our surprise we were released a few minutes later and herded into the changing room where we had to line up. Then Moll announced that *Kapo* Kaminski had been shot. The SS thought that he was planning to assassinate *Oberscharführer* Muhsfeld and that they had succeeded in forestalling him at the last minute. 'And that,' he went on threateningly, 'is precisely what will happen to anybody else who fancies he can pull off a dirty trick like that!'

The news of the shooting of Kaminski came as a severe blow to us all. Dazed and panic-stricken we ran back and forth between changing room and truck, loading gypsy clothing, scarcely able to grasp that we had lost yet another of our best men.

Among the bodies of dead gypsies in the pit waiting to be burned we came across Kaminski's corpse. The SS had taken him to the pit and covered his body with fir branches. He had two bullet holes, one at the back of his neck and another in his left eye which was completely shattered. We never learnt who denounced Kaminski; it was whispered that it was Mietek. For at the request of the Resistance, Kaminski had spoken to Morawa only a few days earlier in order to sound him out discreetly concerning the attitude of the five Polish prisoners in the *Sonderkommando* in case of a rebellion.

When the first flurry about Kaminski's death had somewhat subsided, we began again to worry about the future. We very much feared that in the context of the shooting of Kaminski the SS might have got wind of our escape plans. However, we reasoned that this could not be so, for Moll had talked only of an assassination attempt on *Oberscharführer* Muhsfeld. Besides, it would have been inexplicable why none of the other Resistance leaders had been shot. In the end we came to the conclusion that Moll could not have known about our plans after all.

As the summer of 1944 waned, fewer and fewer transports arrived on the ramp at Birkenau. Suddenly one day *Hauptscharführer* Moll was transferred, apparently to be *Lagerführer* at the auxiliary camp at Gleiwitz.

A few days after his departure there was another selection among *Sonderkommando* prisoners. One afternoon towards the end of September 1944 all prisoners quartered in crematorium 4 had to line up in the yard where *Scharführer* Busch, *Unterscharführer* Gorges and a few SS men of the political department, including *Oberscharführer* Hustek, were waiting. Busch spoke first. He informed us that he needed 200 men for a team in another camp;

accommodation and food there were good, at any rate considerably better than at Birkenau. Then he invited all who wished to join this team to step forward. In the yard there was deathly silence. Not one prisoner moved. Even the ones who had joined the *Sonderkommando* quite recently knew exactly what all this meant. Was Busch really so naïve, I thought, to believe any one of us would volunteer for his own slaughter? A few minutes passed while the SS conferred about what to do next. Then Busch and Gorges stepped forward and began to pick out one prisoner after another, lining them up on the opposite side and noting down their numbers. Almost all who had an 'old' number escaped selection. A little later several armed SS guards led the selected prisoners away.

During the following night our forebodings became certainty. For the first time in the history of Auschwitz SS men took over the duties of *Sonderkommando* prisoners in crematorium 2 in order to cremate the corpses of prisoners selected that afternoon. From fellow prisoners quartered in the loft of the crematorium we learnt what happened that night. To begin with they were strictly forbidden to set foot on the stairs. Allegedly the SS were going to burn the corpses of a large number of civilians who had died during an air raid. However, next morning when the stokers went downstairs in order to get the ovens ready they found that the SS had been less efficient in disposing of the gassed bodies than they might have wished. In some of the ovens they discovered half-charred corpses which they were able to identify.

When this news circulated we were once more overcome by despair and despondency. What would happen to us now that fewer and fewer transports were arriving on the ramp? As long as the death factories were still working flat out we did not have to fear for our lives. But now no one was certain any longer whether tomorrow might not bring another selection; mass extermination in bunker 5 had ceased altogether. For some time now no corpses had been burnt in the pits behind crematorium 5. But the ovens in this crematorium were operating again.

As we had feared there was another selection. It came on 7 October. A few days earlier *Scharführer* Busch had called together the crematorium 5 and bunker 5 *Kapo*s and informed them that he needed 300 men for a rubble clearance team. They were allegedly to be employed in an Upper Silesian town which had been badly damaged by enemy bombs. Busch requested the *Kapo*s to let him have a list with the names and numbers of 300 prisoners within twenty-four hours. Making things easy for himself he had shifted the decision over life and death of 300 people on to the *Kapos*. But he had also placed our *Kapos* in a desperate and hopeless position. For, on the one hand, they could not let all of us live; on the other hand, every name they put on the list made them forcibly responsible for that person's fate. After prolonged discussions and a sleepless night they decided not to put on the list the names of men who, in case of a rebellion, would most readily be in a position to save the lives of others. In the first instance these were the old and experienced prisoners who had proved their reliability several times.

But then what? What was to be the criterion by which one prisoner would have preference over another? 'Old' prisoners argued with the *Kapos*, trying to intervene on behalf of a friend or close work-mate in order to save their lives. I, too, pleaded urgently for two Hungarian doctors. In vain. I was informed that I was lucky my own life was not in jeopardy and, what was more, that nothing much could be expected from highly strung people like the two doctors in case of an emergency. After a long and dramatic night the list bearing 300 names and numbers was finished towards dawn. The names of the unfortunate prisoners on the list were soon known to everyone. None of the wretched men believed a single word of what Busch had given as the reason for drawing up the list.

The 300 prisoners selected by the *Kapos* were mainly Hungarian and Greek Jews. Even before the list was handed to Busch, some of these selected prisoners contacted our Resistance leaders and declared that not one of the 300 was prepared to let himself be slaughtered without resistance. They thought the time for the planned rebellion was now and requested the entire *Sonderkommando* to throw in their lot with them, and to do so whether or not the rest of the camp were to join in. They went on to say that they were determined to go it alone if nobody was prepared to support them. Towards midday the food carriers informed our Resistance contact men in the camp of the events in the crematorium. Their answer was waiting for them when they returned to fetch the evening meal. Any uprising, the message went, was to be avoided at all costs because it might have disastrous consequences for the whole camp. In turn our Resistance leaders explained the situation to the men on the selection list, namely, that we all appreciated their position but could not participate in any violent measure and that the Resistance in the camp shared this view.

Two days came and went after the handing over of the list. Nothing happened. The 300 men were on tenter-hooks and tried to hide their growing nervousness behind an increasing bustle of activity. Surreptitiously they began to collect things like rags, wood-alcohol, oil, and other fuel, and to take them concealed under their clothing into crematorium 4. After evening roll-call they made last-minute preparations for setting crematorium 4 on fire, by stuffing rags soaked in oil and wood-alcohol in between the rafters and the felt roof, under the three-tier wooden bunks and in the coke store.

The atmosphere during the following twenty-four hours was almost unbearably fraught with suspense, restiveness and hectic activity growing steadily, and the 300 doomed prisoners, aware that their lives were forfeited, growing increasingly impatient. In their heart of hearts they cherished the secret hope that the rest of us might, at the last minute, be persuaded to join them and thus give the signal for the whole camp to rise up.

Next day, 7 October, the sky was blue and cloudless. Towards midday, *Scharführer* Busch, *Unterscharführer* Gorges and several other SS men and guards arrived in the yard in front of crematorium 4. All prisoners were ordered to line up, with the exception of fourteen who were away on their various jobs and who, in any case, were not affected by the selection. Then Busch began calling out the first few numbers on the list, starting with the highest and working his way down to the lowest. Those selected for 'transfer' were made to stand on the opposite side of the yard, those not concerned, once they had been called, were allowed to return to crematorium 5. Since I had the lowest number of all assembled in the yard I was still standing there waiting to be called.

Now and then when Busch called a number nobody stepped forward, although he would repeat the number loud and clear. When shortly before the end of the selection there was only a small group of about ten men left, it struck Busch that something was amiss, and that at least a dozen prisoners must be hiding somewhere. He therefore despatched a few of the guards to crematorium 4 to try and track them down. The guards were just leaving when quite suddenly from out of the ranks of selected prisoners they were pelted with a hail of stones. Some SS men were wounded, but others managed to dodge the stones and were drawing their guns and starting to shoot blindly into the crowd of prisoners. Two more SS men had managed to get away to the camp street where they grabbed two bicycles leaning against the camouflage fence and sped off in the direction of the camp.

Meanwhile crematorium 4 had been set on fire, the roof was blazing in several places, flames leaping out and clouds of smoke rising into the sky. Within five minutes of the start of the fighting the camp siren began to wail. Shortly afterwards several trucks arrived, and steel-helmeted SS guards, many of them still in their vests, spilled out: swiftly they surrounded the yard and set up their machine-guns.

All this time I was still in the yard where prisoners were now milling about aimlessly and panic-stricken while from all sides they were met by a shower of bullets. One by one they fell to the ground fatally injured. Finally a large number raced towards the barbed wire to try and break through. I ran to crematorium 4 and a few metres away from the door threw myself to the ground. The shooting continued unabated. I had only one thought: to reach the crematorium without getting hurt. Taking my courage in both hands I stood up, bounded forward and flung myself through the door into the cremation room. I was by now completely out of breath. The crematorium was still burning fiercely. The wooden doors were ablaze, several of the wooden beams were charred and dangling from the ceiling, and there was a fire raging in the coke store. The windows on the opposite wall were riddled with bullet holes. Outside the firing continued. Bullets hit the ovens and ricocheted in all directions.

In a flash I remembered a place where I would be safe from bullets: inside the flue leading from the ovens to the chimney. I lifted one of the cast-iron covers, climbed down and closed the cover behind me. Inside the flue there was no room to stand upright; I stretched out trying to catch my breath. From outside I could still hear the rattle of machine-guns. When after a while the shooting seemed to die down I crawled towards the chimney because I was able to stand up there. As I glanced up I glimpsed, framed by the four soot-blackened chimney walls, a small square of deep blue sky. Still trembling with agitation I lit a cigarette and blew the smoke up into the huge chimney. As it drifted up I suddenly remembered the very many human beings whose mortal remains had gone the same way.

The lull outside did not last long, but was abruptly broken by many different noises. I gathered that the SS were trying to put out the fire. I, too, felt a few splashes of water as it poured down from above so I crawled back into the flue and stayed there for some time. After a while I climbed out of my hiding place and cautiously made my way to one of the windows from where I could overlook the front yard. Down in the yard many of my fellow prisoners were lying very still in their blood-stained prison uniforms. Some SS men were running about with their carbines kicking the prostrate bodies to see whether they were still moving; if there was a slight movement or twitching they emptied several bullets into the victim until he was still.

I thought it advisable to go back to my hiding place and wait until the coast was quite clear. I considered what I ought to do now. True, I had escaped the massacre in the yard but how on earth was I to get out of here? I thought about this for a long time, and then decided to wait until it was dark outside. Then I intended to overpower the SS guard of a small gate leading to the general store-room. Next to this gate was a small door which was never locked and through it I could get into the store-room. First I would have to put on the overpowered SS guard's uniform, before disposing of the second SS guard on the further side of the store-room. After that it would be an easy matter to get away under cover of darkness. It was most important not to make a noise while I dealt with the two SS guards which meant that I would have to put them out of action with a single well-aimed blow from behind. My weapon was to be one of the crow-bars used to declinker the oven gratings.

It was about midnight when I emerged from the flue. This seemed to me the most opportune moment for carrying out my plan. The cremation room roof was burnt out. Looking about me I was struck by the thought that there was at least one death factory put out of action for good. Quietly I crept to the coke store and selected a crow-bar. Then I made my way to the door leading to the back yard and cautiously opened it an inch or two. I peered outside, but there was nothing unusual to see and all was quite quiet. A pale moon cast its light over the landscape; the stars glittered coldly in the sky. I crawled outside on my belly: it was so intensely quiet that I could hear myself breathing. Cautiously I began to crawl along the crematorium wall dragging the heavy crow-bar behind me in my right hand. After each metre I paused and looked about me. On my left was the barbed-wire fence which separated crematorium 4 from the general store-room. Behind I saw the outlines of the deserted wooden barracks, sparsely lit by an arc-lamp. They were crammed with things like clothes, underwear and trunks. Behind me the searchlight beams, their giant fingers moving back and forth across camp B2. Everything was going on just as usual.

Nearer and nearer to the gate I crept. The moon showed me the way but, of course, it also lit up the site for the SS guards. Everything seemed to be going according to plan. Now and then I paused briefly to rest and look round. I had come about two-thirds of the way when suddenly I heard a noise. I lay perfectly still, straining my ears in the direction from which the sound had come. Looking more closely I saw quite clearly the figures of several SS sentries, walking up and down by the gate and talking. My heart began to thump. I realized that I would no longer be able to carry out my plan. Clearly what had happened was that, following today's events, the SS had been put on full alert and the guards reinforced. I had no choice but to withdraw as silently as possible. Perhaps by tomorrow things would have returned to normal. I crept back the way I had come and climbed once more into my hiding place which seemed to me to be the safest spot at that moment. Before long I was fast asleep.

I was awoken by voices and noises coming from the cremation room. After a few moments' listening I thought I could detect our *Kapo*'s voice. Lifting up the iron cover a little I peeped out and there was the *Kapo* standing by the ovens. I lifted the cover completely and asked the *Kapo* what was going on outside. He beckoned me to come out, which I did. Out in the yard I mingled with a group of prisoners who were busy moving a trolley loaded with corpses to crematorium 5. I suppose I looked rather grimy and covered in soot, for the *Kapo* suggested that I should go and have a good wash. He brought me a clean uniform, and after I had freshened up I went outside and rejoined the other prisoners.

When I came face to face with several SS *Unterführer*s, among them Busch and Gorges, my heart sank. What would happen if they recognized me? But I need not have worried; the SS men took no notice of me at all, but took it for granted that I belonged to the group of prisoners working in the yard. Most probably they were still not quite clear about how many prisoners had died in the previous day's shooting. I estimated that there must have been about 200.

In the evening a few trucks piled high with corpses arrived at the crematorium. We were shocked to see that the 250 dead were in fact fellow prisoners who had worked in crematoria 2 and 3. Their prison uniforms were soaked with blood and riddled with bullet holes. Later I learned what had happened to them on the previous day.

When after the attack on the SS men in crematorium 4, the siren began to wail only prisoners not affected by the selection were on the site of crematoria 2 and 3. Seeing the flames leaping up and hearing the shooting the men believed that they too were in serious danger. To begin with Russian prisoners of war seized their hated chief *Kapo* and burnt him alive in one of the ovens. In the meantime, other prisoners were trying to get hold of the *Kommandoführer* with the intention of making him suffer the same fate. However, he had grown suspicious and escaped. When subsequently they saw armed SS guards approaching and beginning to surround the two crematorium buildings they decided on a break-out. The three hand-grenades and the arms *organized* over many months were hastily taken from their hiding-places. With insulated pliers they cut the barbed wire in several places whereupon a large crowd intent on escaping pushed through. Meanwhile SS guards were converging on them from all sides. Suddenly someone threw a hand-grenade at the SS. As it went off there was great confusion among the SS men, for it had caught them completely unawares. The prisoners took advantage of this moment of surprise to escape through the holes in the barbed wire.

Some did manage to break through the outer cordon and to make their way for a few kilometres in the direction of Rajsko. Very soon, however, they met with resistance from SS troops in the neighbourhood who had surrounded them. The fugitives barricaded themselves in a barn. There was a violent gunfight during which the barn went up in flames. The fire spread so rapidly that the fugitives were forced to quit their refuge and face the enemy in the open. Although they used every weapon at their disposal it was an unequal fight, the SS being armed with machine-guns and other automatic weapons. Thus the rebels had no choice but to fight to the last cartridge.

The few who had survived the massacre, although gravely

wounded, managed to report with satisfaction that they had killed or wounded several SS men during the gun battle. It became known later that when awarding the Iron Cross to several SS men the *Lagercommandant* had mentioned that this was the first time concentration camp guards had prevented a mass break-out, a feat of bravery for which their *Führer* had decorated them.

About 450 of our comrades had died during the last twenty-four hours, although Busch had requested no more than 300 names. But these 450 men had fought bravely and died honourably, refusing to resign themselves meekly to their fate. They had been ready to defend their lives to their last breath, a unique event in the history of Auschwitz.

One crematorium had been destroyed. A few SS men had died, a few more had been wounded. It was not enough to stop the extermination machinery. Even if every gas chamber and every oven had been blown up it would have achieved hardly anything; for the extermination technique started by Moll had proved that crematoria were not of decisive importance: pits would do the job just as well.

A few days after the rebellion the political department arrested twelve of our companions and had them taken away. We never learnt anything about their fate. These arrests gave rise to renewed unrest and numerous rumours. Since most of us were in on the plans for an uprising, each one lived in fear of being the next victim of the Gestapo. After the bloody drama of the last few days and the arrest of the twelve the number of prisoners left in the *Sonderkommando* had been reduced to about 200. Of these 170 were quartered in the lofts of crematoria 2 and 3, the rest in crematorium 5.

The hot summer had ended and now it was autumn. For some time now pits had not been used for burning corpses, but the three crematoria were once more operating. It was at this time that work began in connection with covering all traces of the summer's mass exterminations. A newly formed demolition team was engaged in filling up pits, levelling sites, removing huge heaps of ashes, taking away camouflage hurdles, planting trees and laying turf.

Transports of Jews from Theresienstadt and Slovakia, and of gypsies, kept arriving on the ramp, although no longer daily. Most of them were gassed, as were also numbers of *Mussulmans* from the camp. Among these arrivals were three people from my home town, one of whom told me that my uncle had been shot a few days earlier in the forest of Sered. Now I knew that of all my family I was the sole survivor.

The last gassing in Birkenau took place in November 1944: the Soviet army was drawing closer from day to day. Conditions inside the camp began to change fundamentally. All was quiet on the ramp, there was no whistling of engines, no squeaking of brakes, and in the camp street trucks were seen only rarely. Even the SS no longer seemed to be altogether sure of themselves and tended to worry about how they ought to behave. For some weeks now they had been showing signs of fear and uncertainty. It was during these days that they started to burn in the crematorium ovens prisoners' documents, card indexes, death certificates and scores of other documents. Everything pointed to the rule of the Third Reich drawing to a close.

Towards the end of November 1944 the dismantling of crematoria 2 and 3 began. At the same time there was a final selection among members of the *Sonderkommando*. All prisoners in the team were lined up in the yard of crematorium 2. This time the camp authorities had taken precautions to prevent a repetition of events during the previous selection. Hundreds of armed SS guards with a large number of dogs stood behind the barbed-wire fence. The political department was represented by *Unterführer*s Boger and Hustek who, together with the *Kommandoführer*s were in charge of the selection.

For a start, the three pathologists and their assistants were sent to one side and after them the thirty prisoners, including myself, billeted in crematorium 5. Finally the SS chose a third group of some seventy prisoners who were to form the demolition team. The rest were told they would be transferred to camp Grossrosen. What happened to them we never learned, but we all realized that their time had come.

Suddenly from out of the ranks of doomed prisoners stepped the young Rabbinical student who had worked in the hair-drying team. He turned to *Oberscharführer* Muhsfeld and with sublime courage told him to be quiet. Then he began to speak to the crowd: 'Brothers!' he cried, 'it is God's unfathomable will that we are to lay down our lives. A cruel and accursed fate has compelled us to take part in the extermination of our people, and now we are ourselves to become dust and ashes. No miracle has happened. Heaven has sent no avenging bolts of lightning. No rain has fallen strong enough to extinguish the funeral pyres built by the hand of man. We must submit to the inevitable with Jewish resignation. It will be the last trial sent to us by heaven. It is not for us to question the reasons, for we are as nothing before Almighty God. Be not afraid of death! Even if we could, by some chance, save our lives, what use would that be to us now? In vain we would search for our murdered relatives. We should be alone, without a family, without relatives, without friends, without a place we might call our own, condemned to roam the world aimlessly. For us there would be neither rest nor peace of mind until one day we would die in some corner, lonely and forsaken. Therefore, brothers, let us now go to meet death bravely and with dignity!'

The SS did not interrupt him while he spoke. When he had finished there was complete silence among the selected men. The sight of muzzles aimed at them from all sides had convinced them very forcibly of the futility of any resistance and the words they had just heard only underlined the hopelessness of their situation. Among this desperate crowd of men I recognized Dr Pach, most selfless and devoted of doctors, as well as the two dental mechanics whose job had been to melt down the gold taken from the mouths of the dead. As long as they were in the *Sonderkommando* they had consciously existed like corpses waiting their turn. And now the time they had dreaded, the hour they had hoped and prayed would pass them by, had come at last. I, too, felt wretched and depressed for, though so far I had managed to slip through the selection net, I knew it could not be long before my turn would come.

Once the gassings had finally ceased, only one crematorium was kept working, burning the corpses of prisoners who had died in the .main and auxiliary camps. In the same building behind a wooden partition was the dissecting room where Dr Mengele and his assistants continued with their pseudo-medical experiments.

One of the tasks of the demolition team was to empty the remaining ash pits. After the ashes had been tipped into the Vistula, the pits were filled up and covered with turf. We noted with alarm that the seventy demolition team prisoners had been quartered back inside the camp, whereas the thirty of us still lived in crematorium 5. Why, we wondered, were they allowed to go back and move about freely while we were not? It seemed to have sinister implications, but we were unable to put our finger on precisely what the reason for our continued and complete isolation could be.

All this time our living conditions deteriorated steadily. As, with no more transports arriving, we were totally dependent on the meagre fare of the camp kitchen, we were forced to use our small hoards of diamonds, gold and the odd dollar note to barter for foodstuffs and cigarettes until we had nothing left to offer. Accustomed to doing black-market deals with us, the SS guards on the other side of the barbed-wire kept approaching anybody coming within earshot to find out whether they had any gold or diamonds in exchange for which they offered bread, sausage, margarine, cigarettes, tobacco and vodka. All we could do in response to such tempting offers was to shrug our shoulders regretfully. However, help was at hand.

One of the assistants working for Dr Mengele with whom I had struck up a friendship had a brain-wave and let me in on his plan. He asked me to *organize* all the brass I could lay my hands on. This was no problem since in the store-room there was a considerable number of electric light-bulbs whose sockets and screw threads were, of course, made of brass.

With the help of this brass and my assistance he skilfully produced what looked exactly like real gold teeth. Armed with several of these fakes I made my way to the barbed wire, bent on getting rid of them there. The SS men knew that any prisoner sidling up to the barbed-wire fence intended to do business. As soon as I approached with some hesitation the SS guard walking up and down asked me what I had to offer. I indicated that I had a few gold teeth and inquired what he could offer in exchange. He had, I was delighted to learn, bread, sausage and cigarettes.

My mouth watered at the thought of a loaf of bread and a piece of sausage. Nor was I altogether averse to the idea of a few packets of cigarettes. All I had to do was to keep my cool: the guard must on no account be allowed to suspect that there was anything fishy about this deal. Through the barbed wire I thrust a handful of fake gold teeth under his nose and noted his interest in these desirable objects. He was obviously convinced that for a few packets of cigarettes, a loaf of bread and a little sausage he would succeed in diddling me out of a goodly amount of gold; for he disappeared into his watch-tower and returned quite soon with a bulging haversack, inviting me to throw my gold teeth across the fence. I pointed out that, since I was in his power rather than he in mine, and since I was unable to run away without having kept my side of the bargain, I expected him to let me have the things he had promised in exchange first. He seemed to appreciate my argument and handed over a sausage, a loaf and a few packets of cigarettes. I flung my gold teeth across and, afraid my deception might be discovered immediately, ran back into the crematorium, relaxing only when I had closed the door behind me.

Needless to say the rest of the prisoners living in the crematorium soon noticed the two of us smoking cigarettes. They started to watch us like hawks and before long they had cottoned on to our little game with the gold teeth. Once the mystery of their manufacture had been discovered, a frantic hunt for brass began. There was a veritable 'gold rush' and few prisoners did not join in this profitable activity. When there was not a trace of brass left in crematorium 5, we obtained fresh supplies from the remaining crematoria which were being dismantled.

It seemed incredible even to us that this brisk trade with fake gold teeth went on without any of us being found out. But, strange though it may seem, none of the SS men ever suspected that the 'gold' which they had acquired illegally and at some considerable risk might be a few carats short. As for us, we were grateful that by a stroke of genius Mengele's assistant had succeeded in considerably easing our harsh living conditions.

The number of corpses sent to our crematorium for burning grew smaller and smaller. As there were now three gas chambers standing idle, one of the *Kommandoführers* whose family lived in Auschwitz hit upon the idea of housing his many rabbits in their hutches there.

There was now every indication that there was some truth in the rumour that the *Reichsführer* of the SS had ordered the extermination of the Jews to stop. But this afforded little comfort to us in the *Sonderkommando*. We knew from past selections that any member of our team no longer of use as a slave would be ruthlessly done away with. Moreover, we realized that operations in crematorium 5 could be kept going with only half the thirty prisoners working there at present.

In the meantime winter had arrived. The first snow had fallen and covered everything with a white blanket. During the Christmas holidays all was quiet in the camp and also in the crematorium. It was a peace which was short-lived. A few days later we heard the news that in the women's camp four young girls had been hanged in front of the assembled prisoners. They were Jewesses who had smuggled the explosives out of the Union munitions factory which were used during the October revolt. At the same time the five Polish prisoners in the *Sonderkommando*, including Mietek, were transferred to another camp. I learned later that a few days before the end of the war they were shot in Mauthausen.

The blanket of snow was getting thicker and the cold more severe, while the muted and distant grumbling of cannons grew slowly louder. We estimated that the front could only be 50 to 80 kilometres away. It was interesting to watch the SS men, nervous and apprehensive, attempting to act professionally and yet oozing affability.

However, it was not only the authority of the SS, but also that of block seniors, *Kapos* and their minions, which disintegrated. Discipline slackened, orders were ignored or carried out casually and with reluctance: this would have been unthinkable only a few days before. In the camp nothing any longer worked as efficiently as before. In the crematorium we noticed that corpses of prisoners who had died in the camp were no longer brought in at certain times daily, but only every few days at irregular intervals, no doubt owing to a shortage of vehicles.

And then came that memorable 18 January 1945. There was great confusion throughout the camp. Early in the morning columns of smoke could be seen rising in all parts of the camp. Quite obviously the SS men were destroying card indexes and other documents. The prisoners who normally at this time of day were bustling about, seemed almost paralysed with inaction: not a single team left the camp for work. The rumble of guns and the explosions of heavy shelling were very close, SS men on bikes and motor cycles were dashing back and forth on the snow-covered camp street where, not long ago, long columns of men, women and children had dragged themselves along to their deaths.

Certain that today we must die we watched the three SS men in the crematorium – Gorges, Kurschuss and another *Unterführer* – with eagle eyes. In the end everything turned out quite differently. In the course of the late afternoon a *Blockführer* came running to the crematorium and shouted nervously: 'Return to camp, everybody! At the double!' We did not need to be told twice and ran right across the copse back to camp B2d where our mates from the demolition team had been quartered for some weeks. Chaos reigned here too; nobody knew what was going on. But evening roll-call did take place; it was to be the last one in

Auschwitz. Thousands of us had lined up. For the first time I had the feeling of being a prisoner like any other. Today we lined up not according to our separate blocks, but any old how. Towards the end of roll-call we were asked to get ready for the transport. Then we were dismissed.

The entire camp was in a turmoil of excitement, with prisoners seized by alarm and euphoria at one and the same time. Everybody tried to *organize* all sorts of things which might come in useful during a lengthy transport in severe weather. Garments waiting to be disinfected, and also the most thoroughly tattered rags, as long as they could be used as protection against the cold, were stolen from *Canada*. At the spot near the camp gate where the orchestra used to play the prisoners' card index went up in flames. Everywhere confusion was at its height.

Then, before midnight, the order to march was given. It was an exhilarating moment. Outside it was snowing and very cold. Some 20,000 prisoners formed up in a long marching column and, flanked by armed SS guards, set out into the night. The snow crunched under our feet, a cold wind blew into our faces. We talked about nothing but where they were taking us and what they intended to do with us.

We marched intermittently for a few days until we came to Loslau where we were herded into open railway cattle trucks. Many people did not survive this long march in the bitter cold, without hot food or drink and without warm clothes. The physically weak and the sick lasted only a few hours. Anyone too exhausted to go on was shot by the guards and left by the wayside. Several prisoners managed to escape under cover of darkness.

The long march across the snow-covered landscape gave me a chance to ponder the events of the last few days. I still could not quite grasp that I had really left Auschwitz. Again and again I asked myself why we, the last few remaining *Sonderkommando* prisoners, had not been shot before the evacuation. Then again I told myself that I should not be marching in this column but for my indomitable will to survive; that I had to thank chance and a kindly fate for escaping one *Sonderkommando* selection after another. And finally I remembered those brave Czech girls who threw me out of the gas chamber when I had wanted to end my life. I tried to imagine what it would be like to be a free man again, in a world without barbed wire, without gas chambers, and without hecatombs of corpses. I wondered what the world would say when I told them the horrific story of how I had spent the last few years.

In the open cattle trucks, exposed to the biting cold, we travelled for several days from Loslau to Mauthausen. We were strictly forbidden to leave our trucks. No rations were handed out. Under these harsh conditions it was not surprising that many died from cold or hunger during the transport. Some tried to escape by jumping from the moving train during the night, risking not only injury but also being picked off by the SS who had machine-guns and swivelling searchlights set up all along the train. When at long last our arduous transport arrived at the little station of Mauthausen in Lower Austria, we were taken to the concentration camp which was not far away. As we marched through the camp gate no one knew how many had escaped, died or been killed since the evacuation of Auschwitz.

Dressed reasonably warmly with fairly decent shoes I had survived the transport comparatively well. I even had a little bread left from the hoard of food I had *organized* before we departed.

In the new camp everything proceeded in the usual tedious way. As we were new arrivals we had to go through the whole routine of shower, disinfection, quartering, roll-calls, and all the rest of concentration camp harassment. On the third day after our arrival we had lined up for roll-call in the late afternoon, when out of the blue one of the *SS-Unterführer*s gave the order: 'All prisoners of the Auschwitz *Sonderkommando*, fall out!' I felt as though someone had punched me in the pit of the stomach. At first I was quite petrified, my heart thumping wildly in my chest. But soon I recovered my composure. Nothing happened. When the order was repeated, there was again no reaction. No one moved, no one stepped forward. The order was repeated a third time, but once more there was no result.

From the corner of my eye I watched our two *Sonderkommando Kapos* and the rest of our team. All of them were standing in their ranks, trying to look inconspicuous and not to betray with one bat of an eyelid that the command had been addressed to them. When there had been no reaction whatever to his three orders the *SS-Unterführer* who, of course, did not know any of us, marched up and down several times, looking searchingly at a few men, no doubt in an attempt to intimidate them. This sudden interest displayed in the survivors of the *Sonderkommando* was not very welcome to any of us, and it certainly put a damper on my hopes.

Roll-call seemed to go on forever. When all attempts to get us to step forward had failed we were dismissed. But the order 'All prisoners of the Auschwitz *Sonderkommando*, fall out!' still rang in my ears.

A few days later a few hundred of us were transferred to the auxiliary camp in Melk where we were set to work digging tunnels into the hillside to provide accommodation for local production plants. The work was hard and strenuous and working conditions arduous and fraught with danger owing to the total absence of safety precautions. Workers were continually getting hurt by rock or earth falls or by falling off the primitive wooden scaffolding. In addition, we were not given enough to eat. Day by day I could feel myself growing weaker and I worried how much longer I would be able to stand this heavy labour.

One evening during roll-call there was an appeal for trained electricians. Taught by long experience that in a concentration camp the life of a trained craftsman was invariably much easier than that of an unskilled labourer, I volunteered without a moment's hesitation. On the following day the electricians – of whom, although wholly ignorant of their trade, I was now one – left for the auxiliary camp of Gusen 1. During the journey I fell into conversation with a Frenchman who was a skilled electrician. We agreed to work together and he promised to show me the ropes whenever possible. Our new place of work was a large assembly shop in the Messerschmitt aircraft factory where we worked on electrical installations inside the fuselage of jacked-up aeroplanes.

Meanwhile April had arrived, and everything was in the process of disintegration. Railway tracks had been destroyed and the roads were under constant attack from low-flying aeroplanes, resulting in a complete standstill of rail and road transport. Nevertheless we continued working in two shifts. I need not have worried that my total ignorance of the electrician's trade might show me up for, since aircraft no longer left the assembly shop, we had practically no work and spent our time standing about idly under the aircraft. All of us realized that the collapse of the Third Reich was only a few days away. But days can seem interminable when one feels the pangs of hunger: in desperation we were driven to eating lubricating jelly, grass, and even the heavy, rich soil.

The last phase of our prisoner existence had begun. Once more we had to muster our remaining strength and energy in order not to die from hunger and exhaustion at the last minute.

The unceasing attacks by Allied aircraft meant that we were spending most of our time in the air-raid tunnel a few hundred metres from the assembly shop where, as soon as the siren went, SS guards would herd us to the accompaniment of the usual curses and blows. One day when I was just about to sprint across to the shelter, *Unterscharführer* Gorges stood suddenly in front of me, his truncheon held high, shouting 'Come along, come along, into the shelter, quickly!' Then he recognized me and stopped in mid-blow to let me run on. I ran as fast as I could into the tunnel and slunk away into a corner because I had no wish to encounter Gorges again. The question going round and round in my brain, was having recognized me, did he intend to give me away? Nothing untoward happened until two days later he suddenly loomed up in front of me like a spectre. He inquired how I was getting on and generally behaved as if nothing was amiss. Having recovered from the initial shock I perked up and thought that I might as well drop a gentle hint to the effect that I had nothing to eat and would not say no to a little bread. However, at the back of my mind I still had that nagging worry that Gorges might give me away to the camp authorities. Next morning, much to my amazement, there he was again, complete with half a loaf of bread and a handful of tobacco. Why he never informed against me has remained a mystery to this day.

A few days later the camp was evacuated. Before we left, everyone was given a bread ration. And then we set out on our march, in a cloud of dust and escorted by large numbers of SS guards. We had not been told where we were making for, but judging from the position of the sun we were marching in a south-westerly direction.

After only a few kilometres the first few collapsed. Anybody unable to get up was immediately shot. Even now, when their time was so obviously almost up, the SS took care to remove every last trace of their crimes. After the first few corpses had been flung onto the side of the road, an *SS-Unterführer* ordered ten men, including me, to step aside. We were told to wait by the roadside.

Meanwhile the last stragglers in the column had dragged themselves past the spot where we were still waiting in the company of the *Unterführer* who did not deign to speak to us. After an hour a horse-drawn vehicle appeared from the direction in which the column had disappeared. The driver, an elderly member of the *Volkssturm**, reversed and stopped. We were ordered to load the corpses on his vehicle. With his cart piled high with bodies he drove to the cemetery in the next town. There a largish grave had been dug in the meantime into which we threw the nameless corpses. Then we continued on our way in the wake of the marching column. I mused wryly on the strange fate which had once more put me in a team whose job was the removal of corpses.

As we passed through a village or hamlet with our giant hearse the inhabitants, as soon as they set eyes on its grisly load, turned away in horror and disappeared into their houses. One could see that many felt sorry for us and would have liked to help. Outside a few of the houses small heaps of apples, carrots and bread had been placed which we picked up and devoured ravenously. When I had eaten my fill I decided to lay in a small store. From a barn I took a piece of cord which I tied round my waist. Then I stuffed anything edible I could find inside my shirt so that nothing could fall out. The next few days were to prove that I had done the right thing.

Our march ended in a wood not far from Gunskirchen near Wels, inside a few wooden barracks surrounded by watch-towers. There was not an SS man in sight. We had no roll-call, did no work. Now and then a few cauldrons of soup appeared. Of discipline there was not a trace. Lying on the barracks' floors were hundreds of emaciated forms, apathetically drowsing and looking as if the last spark of life had departed from them.

I had taken up residence in one of the barracks, perched on a narrow rafter, strapping myself in with a belt so as not to have to keep holding my balance, and covering myself with a blanket. There was, needless to say, never any question of proper sleep. Below me the moaning and groaning continued day and night. Dead bodies lay strewn all over the place, no one concerning themselves with their removal: the stench took one's breath away. Besides, I had to take care not to make a wrong movement, or else I might have fallen 3 metres. It was here that the wisdom of hoarding food inside my shirt became apparent. Of course, if the others had discovered my secret supplies I should have been lost. Thus I only dared to eat in the dark, chewing my precious food slowly and, most important, noiselessly. With alarm I watched my little hoard getting smaller every day.

Despite the adverse conditions under which all of us suffered, there were rumours galore. One minute the Americans were only

50 kilometres away, while a few minutes later Allied armoured spear-heads were reported 80 kilometres off. One rumour followed hard upon the other, but no one knew what was actually happening.

My physical and spiritual state of health was deteriorating rapidly. Still lying precariously perched on my rafter, I watched rather impassively as scores of lice were walking all over my blanket. I scarcely any longer noticed the moaning and groaning in the barrack below me. I felt somnolent, as though I was just about to drop off to sleep. Then all of a sudden from all around us there came the noise of fighting. The chattering of machine-guns and the bursting of shells made me feel wide awake. Before long people burst into the barrack, their arms raised, and shouting exuberantly: 'We are free! Comrades, we are free!'

It was, incredibly, a complete anti-climax. This moment, on which all my thought and secret wishes had been concentrated for three years, evoked neither gladness nor, for that matter, any other feelings inside me. I let myself drop down from my rafter and crawled on all fours to the door. Outside I struggled along a little further, but then I simply stretched out on a woodland ground and fell fast asleep.

I awoke to the monotonous noise of vehicles rumbling past. Walking across to the near by road I saw a long column of American tanks clanking along in the direction of Wels. As I stared after the convoy of steel giants I realized that the hideous Nazi terror had ended at last.

Appendix:
Plans of Auschwitz

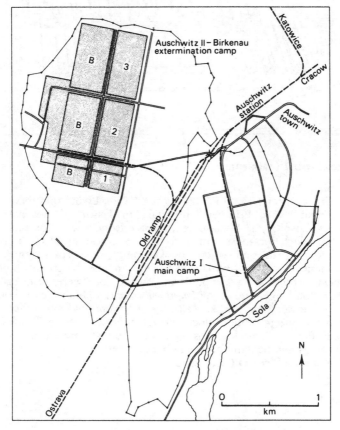

Auschwitz II – Birkenau
extermination camp

B 3

Auschwitz
station

Katowice

Cracow

Auschwitz
town

B 2

B 1

Old ramp

Auschwitz I
main camp

Sola

N

Ostrava

0   1
km

1   Layout of Auschwitz

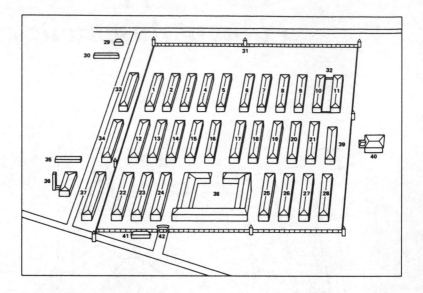

2   Auschwitz I main camp

Block plan
1–8 Living quarters; 12–18 Living quarters; 22–3 Living quarters; 25–7
Living quarters; 9 Prisoners' hospital; 19 Prisoners' hospital; 21
Prisoners' hospital; 28 Medical centre for prisoners who continued to
work; 20 Block for those with infectious diseases; 24 Block housing
prisoners' records and where bookkeeping on corpses done; 10
Experiment block; 11 Bunkerblock (cells in the basement housed
prisoners who had attempted to escape or were undergoing
interrogation); 29 House of the *Lagerkommandant*; 30 Main guard-house;
31 Watch-tower; 32 'Black wall'; 33 *Lagerkommandant*'s office; 34
Administration; 35 Political block; 36 Old crematorium; 37 SS sick-bay,
camp doctor; 38 Camp kitchens; 39 Annex (served different purposes);
40 'Theatre building' (an unfinished building serving mainly as a store);
41 *Blockführers*' office; 42 Camp gate

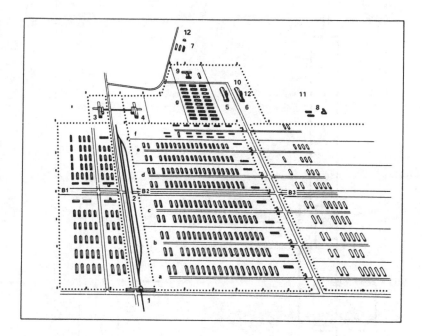

3   Auschwitz II–Birkenau extermination camp

1 Main gate; 2 Ramp; 3 Crematorium 2; 4 Crematorium 3; 5 Crematorium 4; 6 Crematorium 5; 7 Bunker 2 (later Bunker 5), with three changing rooms; 8 Bunker 1, first gas chamber in Birkenau, with two changing rooms; 9 Sauna; 10 Site of cremation pits near Crematorium 5; 11 Site where in 1941–2 thousands of corpses were buried; 12 Site of cremation pits near Bunker 5 in 1944; barbed-wire fence forming the inner cordon; B1 Women's camp; B2a Quarantine camp; B2b Family camp; B2c Women's camp from 1944; B2d Men's camp; B2e Gypsy camp; B2f Prison hospital; B2g *Canada* camp; B3 *Mexico* camp, only partly completed

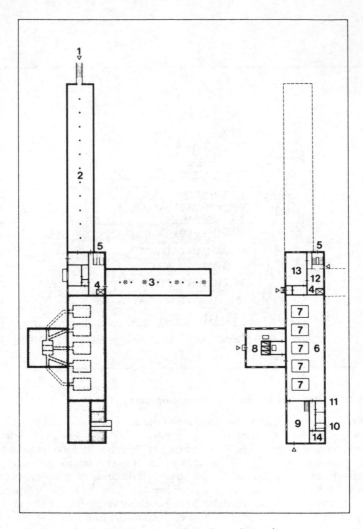

4 **Crematorium** 3 (crematorium 2 a mirror image)

1 Stairs to changing room; 2 Changing room; 3 Gas chamber; ■ concrete pillar; ⊗ gas inlet; 4 Lift for corpses; 5 Chute for remains of corpses; 6 Incineration room; 7 Ovens, each with 3 chambers; 8 Chimney; 9 Coke store; 10 Washroom WC; 11 *Kommandoführer*'s office; 12 Execution room; 13 Room where gold fillings melted down in crematorium 2, dissecting room; 14 In crematorium 3 quarters of those who melted down gold fillings

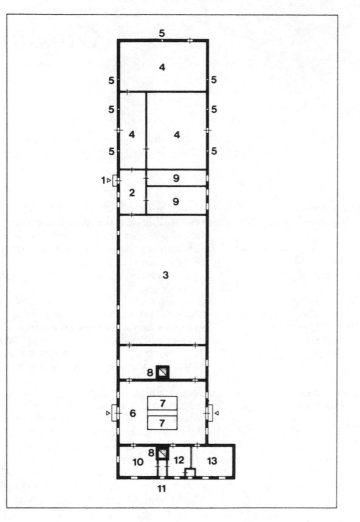

5   Crematorium 5 (crematorium 4 a mirror image)

1 Entrance to the changing room; 2 Ante-room; 3 Changing room;
Execution room; Corpse room; In crematorium 4 from summer 1944
the *Sonderkommando*'s quarters; 4 Gas chamber; 5 Gas inlet; 6
Incineration room; 7 Oven with 4 incineration chambers; 8 Chimney; 9
Sonderkommando's quarters. In crematorium 5 from autumn 1944 quarters
of the *Sonderkommando*; 10 *Kommandoführer*'s office; 11 *Kapo*s'
headquarters; 12 Washroom/WC; 13 Coke store

Glossary

Arbeitsdienste	This consisted of prisoners who were responsible for the distribution of their fellow prisoners to work squads. They also submitted proposals for the appointment of new *Kapos*.
Bar-mitzvah	Confirmation of Jewish boys when 13 years of age.
Block orderly *(Stubendienst)*	Prisoner who had to keep the block clean and tidy. He did not have to work outside in teams like his fellow prisoners.
Block clerk *(Blockschreiber)*	A type of bookkeeper recording data on and movements of all prisoners in the block. He was deputy to the block senior *(Blockältester)*.
Block senior *(Blockältester)*	The leading prisoner of a block and responsible for cleanliness and tidiness. Not doing any work himself he hounded the other prisoners and received a double portion of soup for his pains. He reported to the *Blockführer*.
Blockführer	The block leader was an SS man whose duty was to supervise work in a couple of blocks and to arrange daily reports. He reported to the *Rapportführer*.
Bum-boy *(Piepel)*	A lad corrupted by camp life who served the pleasures of the *Kapos* and block seniors. Sometimes he was sexually abused.
Canada	A name given by Polish prisoners to the section in the camp where the belongings of deported Jews were sorted and stored.

	There, almost anything could be *organized*. Obviously the Poles imagined Canada to be a country of unlimited wealth.
FS Leute (in Slovakia)	Abbreviation of *Freiwillige Schutzstaffel*, volunteer SS.
Funktionshäftling	A prisoner entrusted with special duties by the SS.
Hauptscharführer	Sergeant major.
Hauptsturmführer	Captain.
Kapo	Prisoner of a concentration camp in charge of a working party.
Kommando	Working party or team.
Kommandoführer	SS man supervising a working team of prisoners.
Lagerführer	The SS leader in charge of one or more sections of the camp executing power in matters affecting the prisoners. He was responsible to the *Lagerkommandant*.
Lagerkommandant	The commandant of the entire camp including the SS, directly responsible to Berlin.
Mexico	The name *Mexico* originated in the spring of 1944 when prisoners were quartered in this not quite completed camp without any clothing whatever. They wrapped themselves in coloured blankets which made them look rather like Mexican Indians.
Mussulman	Camp slang for a prisoner who had lost the will to live.
Oberaufseherin	Head wardress.
Oberscharführer	Platoon sergeant.
Obersturmführer	First lieutenant.
Organize	Camp slang meaning to take without permission, to steal, to scrounge.
Ortskommandant	Senior commanding officer of the troops quartered in a town or village.
Political department	Its headquarters was in the main camp of Auschwitz I. This inquisitional organization spied on prisoners, civilian employees and SS alike. Its agents prowled through the camp compounds inspecting everything, and searching unsuspecting prisoners and civilians, and watching for any unauthorized contact between the prisoners and the SS or civilians.

Rapportführer	Directly translated means roll-call leader. An NCO, he was responsible for order, discipline in a particular section of the camp. He reported to the camp administration.
Reichsdeutscher	German citizen, citizen of the Reich (as a geographical unit before 1938).
Rottenführer	Lance corporal.
Scharführer	Lance sergeant.
Selection	In camp parlance this meant selection for extermination.
Sonderbehandlung	(Special Treatment) Top secret code word used by the SS for killing and murdering.
Strafkompanie	Penal or fatigue company.
Sturmmann	Private, first class.
Unterscharführer	Sergeant.
Untersturmführer	SS subaltern with the rank of second lieutenant.
Volksdeutscher	Ethnic German, German of foreign nationality.
Volkssturm	A territorial army formed by the Germans in the latter part of World War 2, consisting of men and boys unfit for regular military service.